TOGETHER IN PEACE

1975

TOGETHER IN PEACE

by
Joseph M. Champlin

AVE MARIA PRESS
NOTRE DAME, INDIANA 46556

FATHER JOSEPH M. CHAMPLIN, former Associate Director, Secretariat, Bishops' Committee on the Liturgy, is Pastor of Holy Family Church, Fulton, New York. He has lectured extensively throughout the country, and his syndicated column appears in 90 Catholic newspapers.

His other works include *Together For Life,* the most popular marriage preparation book in use today (over a million copies in print), *Don't You Really Love Me?* (200,000 in print), *Christ Present And Yet To Come, The Mass In a World of Change,* and *The Sacraments In a World of Change.* In addition, he has appeared on national radio and television, and has recorded several cassettes on liturgy and pastoral life.

First printing, 50,000, April 1975
Second printing, 50,000, July 1975

Nihil Obstat: Rev. John L. Roark
Censor Deputatus
August 22, 1974

Imprimatur: Most Rev. David F. Cunningham, D.D.
Bishop of Syracuse

Acknowledgments
The text of The New American Bible, copyright © 1970 by the Confraternity of Christian Doctrine, Washington, D.C., is reproduced herein by license of said Confraternity of Christian Doctrine. All rights reserved.

English translation of the *Rite of Penance,* copyright © 1974, International Committee on English in the Liturgy, Inc. All rights reserved.

ISBN: 0-87793-095-3

For the priests and penitents
in my life who have sought or
given Christ's healing peace

Contents

Introduction

God has given us the sacrament of Penance so troubled sinners might meet with faith the forgiving Jesus Christ and walk away in peace.

The stronger our faith, the clearer we view our sins, the more honestly we confess them, the greater our desire to improve, the deeper will be the inner joy and personal freedom we experience on those occasions.

This booklet is designed to help in each of these areas. You may follow the text by yourself or together with a priest who wishes to share portions of it with his penitents.

There are five steps which surround and make possible a peaceful meeting with the Lord of mercy. The sections of this book correspond to each of those stages.

Step 1:
Prayer for Light and Courage

We begin by a brief prayer asking God to help us believe in his mercy, to see our sins just as they are, to confess them honestly despite the pain that involves, to experience his peace, and to change our future lives.

This prayer from the heart can be in your own words and thoughts or may be expressed in one of the formulas below:

A.

God our Father in heaven,
send your Holy Spirit into my heart.
Point out my sins.
Supply the courage I need to confess them honestly.
Help me to believe you are always willing to forgive.
Remove my sin and guilt,
fill me with peace,
then send me away strong, free,
and determined I will be better in the days ahead.
I ask for these things through Jesus, your Son,
who is my Lord and Savior.

B. PSALM 6

I

O LORD, reprove me not in your anger,
   nor chastise me in your wrath.
Have pity on me, O LORD, for I am languishing;
   heal me, O LORD, for my body is in terror;
My soul, too, is utterly terrified;
   but you, O LORD, how long . . . ?

II

Return, O LORD, save my life;
    rescue me because of your kindness,
For among the dead no one remembers you;
    in the nether world who gives you thanks?

III

I am wearied with sighing;
    every night I flood my bed with weeping;
    I drench my couch with my tears.
My eyes are dimmed with sorrow;
    they have aged because of all my foes.

IV

Depart from me, all evildoers,
    for the LORD has heard the sound of my weeping;
The LORD has heard my plea;
    the LORD has accepted my prayer.
All my enemies shall be put to shame in utter terror;
    they shall fall back in sudden shame.

C. PSALM 38

I

O LORD, in your anger punish me not,
    in your wrath chastise me not;
For your arrows have sunk deep in me,
    and your hand has come down upon me.
There is no health in my flesh because of your
        indignation;
    there is no wholeness in my bones because of
        my sin,

11

For my iniquities have overwhelmed me;
  they are like a heavy burden, beyond my strength.

II

Noisome and festering are my sores
  because of my folly,
I am stooped and bowed down profoundly;
  all the day I go in mourning,
For my loins are filled with burning pains;
  there is no health in my flesh.
I am numbed and severely crushed;
  I roar with anguish of heart.

O LORD, all my desire is before you;
  from you my groaning is not hid.
My heart throbs; my strength forsakes me;
  the very light of my eyes has failed me.
My friends and my companions stand back because of
    my affliction;
  my neighbors stand afar off.
Men lay snares for me seeking my life;
  they look to my misfortune, they speak of ruin,
  treachery they talk of all the day.

III

But I am like a deaf man, hearing not,
  like a dumb man who opens not his mouth.
I am become like a man who neither hears
  nor has in his mouth a retort.
Because for you, O LORD, I wait;
  you, O Lord my God, will answer
When I say, "Let them not be glad on my account
  who, when my foot slips, glory over me."

IV

For I am very near to falling,
  and my grief is with me always.
Indeed, I acknowledge my guilt;
  I grieve over my sin.
But my undeserved enemies are strong;
  many are my foes without cause.
Those who repay evil for good
  harass me for pursuing good.
Forsake me not, O LORD;
  my God, be not far from me!
Make haste to help me,
  O Lord my salvation!

D. PSALM 130

I

Out of the depths I cry to you, O LORD;
  Lord, hear my voice!
Let your ears be attentive
  to my voice in supplication:

II

If you, O LORD, mark iniquities,
  Lord, who can stand?
But with you is forgiveness,
  that you may be revered.

III

I trust in the LORD;
  my soul trusts in his word.
My soul waits for the LORD
  more than sentinels wait for the dawn.

IV

More than sentinels wait for the dawn,
  let Israel wait for the LORD,
For with the LORD is kindness
  and with him is plenteous redemption;
And he will redeem
  Israel from all their iniquities.

Step 2:
God's Good Words *About* Forgiveness

*The bible is filled with stories and teachings about
God's limitless mercy, love and forgiveness. Read now
one or a few of the selections below and reflect for
several moments upon them.*

A. Matthew 9:9-13 *Jesus' Concern for Sinners*

As he moved on, Jesus saw a man named Matthew
at his post where taxes were collected. He said to
him, "Follow me." Matthew got up and followed
him. Now it happened that, while Jesus was at table
in Matthew's home, many tax collectors and those
known as sinners came to join Jesus and his disciples
at dinner. The Pharisees saw this and complained
to his disciples, "What reason can the Teacher have
for eating with tax collectors and those who disregard
the law?" Overhearing the remark, he said: "People
who are in good health do not need a doctor; sick
people do. Go and learn the meaning of the
words, 'It is mercy I desire and not sacrifice.' I have
come to call, not the self-righteous, but sinners."

B. Luke 5:17-26 *Christ Forgives and Cures the
Paralytic*

One day Jesus was teaching, and the power of the
Lord made him heal. Sitting close by were Pharisees
and teachers of the law who had come from every
village of Galilee and from Judea and Jerusalem.

Some men came along carrying a paralytic on a mat. They were trying to bring him in and lay him before Jesus; but they found no way of getting him through because of the crowd, so they went up on the roof. There they let him down with his mat through the tiles into the middle of the crowd before Jesus. Seeing their faith, Jesus said, "My friend, your sins are forgiven you."

The scribes and the Pharisees began a discussion, saying: "Who is this man who utters blasphemies? Who can forgive sins but God alone?" Jesus, however, knew their reasoning and answered them by saying: "Why do you harbor these thoughts? Which is easier: to say, 'Your sins are forgiven you,' or to say, 'Get up and walk'? In any case, to make it clear to you that the Son of Man has authority on earth to forgive sins"—he then addressed the paralyzed man: "I say to you, get up! Take your mat with you, and return to your house."

At once the man stood erect before them. He picked up the mat he had been lying on and went home praising God. At this they were all seized with astonishment. Full of awe, they gave praise to God, saying, "We have seen incredible things today!"

C. Luke 7:36-50 *The Lord and a Penitent Woman*

There was a certain Pharisee who invited Jesus to dine with him. Jesus went to the Pharisee's home and reclined to eat. A woman known in the town to be a sinner learned that he was dining in the Pharisee's home. She brought in a vase of perfumed oil and stood behind him at his feet, weeping so that her tears fell upon his feet. Then she wiped them with her hair, kissing them and perfuming them with the oil. When his host, the Pharisee, saw this, he said to himself, "If this man were a prophet, he would

16

know who and what sort of woman this is that touches him—that she is a sinner." In answer to his thoughts, Jesus said to him, "Simon, I have something to propose to you." "Teacher," he said, "speak."

"Two men owed money to a certain moneylender; one owed a total of five hundred coins, the other fifty. Since neither was able to repay, he wrote off both debts. Which of them was more grateful to him?" Simon answered, "He, I presume, to whom he remitted the larger sum." Jesus said to him, "You are right."

Turning then to the woman, he said to Simon: "You see this woman? I came to your home and you provided me with no water for my feet. She has washed my feet with her tears and wiped them with her hair. You gave me no kiss, but she has not ceased kissing my feet since I entered. You did not anoint my head with oil, but she has anointed my feet with perfume. I tell you, that is why her many sins are forgiven—because of her great love. Little is forgiven the one whose love is small."

He said to her then, "Your sins are forgiven"; at which his fellow guests began to ask among themselves, "Who is this that he even forgives sins?" Meanwhile he said to the woman, "Your faith has been your salvation. Now go in peace."

D. Luke 15:1-7 *A Story of the Lost Sheep*

The tax collectors and sinners were all gathering around to hear him, at which the Pharisees and the scribes murmured, "This man welcomes sinners and eats with them." Then he addressed this parable to them: "Who among you, if he has a hundred sheep and loses one of them, does not leave the ninety-nine in the wasteland and follow the lost one until he finds it? And when he finds it, he puts it on his shoulders in jubilation. Once arrived home, he invites friends and neighbors in and says to them, 'Rejoice with me because I have found my lost sheep.' I tell you, there will likewise be more joy in heaven over one repentant sinner than over ninety-nine righteous people who have no need to repent.

E. Luke 15:8-10 *The Misplaced Silver Coin*

"What woman, if she has ten silver pieces and loses one, does not light a lamp and sweep the house in a diligent search until she has retrieved what she lost? And when she finds it, she calls in her friends and neighbors to say, 'Rejoice with me! I have found the silver piece I lost.' I tell you, there will be the same kind of joy before the angels of God over one repentant sinner."

F. Luke 15:11-32 *The Wandering and Wasteful Son Who Returned Home*

Jesus said to them: "A man had two sons. The younger of them said to his father, 'Father, give me the share of the estate that is coming to me.' So the father divided up the property. Some days later this younger son collected all his belongings and went off to a distant land, where he squandered his money on dissolute living. After he had spent everything, a great famine broke out in that country and he was in dire need. So he attached himself to one of the propertied class of the place, who sent him to his farm to take care of the pigs. He longed to fill his belly with the husks that were fodder for the pigs, but no one made a move to give him anything. Coming to his senses at last, he said: 'How many hired hands at my father's place have more than enough to eat, while here I am starving! I will break away and return to my father, and say to him, Father, I have sinned against God and against you; I no longer deserve to be called your son. Treat me like one of your hired hands.' With that he set off for his father's house. While he was still a long way off, his father caught sight of him and was deeply moved. He ran out to meet him, threw his arms around his neck, and kissed him. The son said to him, 'Father, I have sinned against God and against you; I no longer deserve to be called your son.' The father said to his servants: 'Quick! bring out the finest robe and put it on him; put a ring on his finger and shoes on his feet. Take the fatted calf and kill it. Let us eat and celebrate, because this son of mine was dead and has come back to life. He was lost and is found.' Then the celebration began.

"Meanwhile the elder son was out on the land. As he neared the house on his way home, he heard the sound of music and dancing. He called one of the servants and asked him the reason for the dancing and the music. The servant answered, 'Your brother is home, and your father has killed the fatted calf because he has him back in good health.' The son grew angry at this and would not go in; but his father came out and began to plead with him.

"He said to his father in reply: 'For years now I have slaved for you. I never disobeyed one of your orders, yet you never gave me so much as a kid goat to celebrate with my friends. Then, when this son of yours returns after having gone through your property with loose women, you kill the fatted calf for him.'

"'My son,' replied the father, 'you are with me always, and everything I have is yours. But we had to celebrate and rejoice! This brother of yours was dead, and has come back to life. He was lost, and is found.' "

G. Luke 19:1-10 *Jesus and Zacchaeus the Tax Collector*

Entering Jericho, he passed through the city. There
was a man there named Zacchaeus, the chief tax
collector and a wealthy man. He was trying to see
what Jesus was like, but being small of stature, was
unable to do so because of the crowd. He first ran on
in front, then climbed a sycamore tree which was
along Jesus' route, in order to see him. When Jesus
came to the spot he looked up and said, "Zacchaeus,
hurry down. I mean to stay at your house today."
He quickly descended, and welcomed him with de-
light. When this was observed, everyone began to
murmur, "He has gone to a sinner's house as a guest."
    Zacchaeus stood his ground and said to the Lord:
"I give half my belongings, Lord, to the poor. If I
have defrauded anyone in the least, I pay him back
fourfold." Jesus said to him: "Today salvation has
come to this house, for this is what it means to be a
son of Abraham. The Son of Man has come to search
out and save what was lost."

H. John 8:1-11 *A Woman Caught in Adultery*

Then each went off to his own house, while
Jesus went out to the Mount of Olives. At
daybreak he reappeared in the temple area; and when
the people started coming to him, he sat down and
began to teach them. The scribes and the Pharisees
led a woman forward who had been caught in
adultery. They made her stand in front of everyone.
"Teacher," they said to him, "this woman has been
caught in the act of adultery. In the law, Moses
ordered such women to be stoned. What do you have
to say about the case?" (They were posing this ques-
tion to trap him, so that they could have something

to accuse him of.) Jesus bent down and started tracing on the ground with his finger. When they persisted in their questioning, he straightened up and said to them, "Let the man among you who has no sin be the first to cast a stone at her." A second time he bent down and wrote on the ground. Then the audience drifted away one by one, beginning with the elders. This left him alone with the woman, who continued to stand there before him. Jesus finally straightened up and said to her, "Woman, where did they all disappear to? Has no one condemned you?" "No one, sir," she answered. Jesus said, "Nor do I condemn you. You may go. But from now on, avoid this sin."

I. John 20:19-23 *Christ's Easter Gift of Peace and Forgiveness*

On the evening of that first day of the week, even though the disciples had locked the doors of the place where they were for fear of the Jews, Jesus came and stood before them. "Peace be with you," he said. When he had said this, he showed them his hands and his side. At the sight of the Lord the disciples rejoiced. "Peace be with you," he said again.

"As the Father has sent me, so I send you." Then he breathed on them and said: "Receive the Holy Spirit. If you forgive men's sins, they are forgiven them; if you hold them bound, they are held bound."

J. Romans 5:6-11 *The Lord Died for Our Sins*

At the appointed time, when we were still powerless, Christ died for us godless men. It is rare that anyone should lay down his life for a just man, though it is barely possible that for a good man someone may have the courage to die. It is precisely in this that

God proves his love for us; that while we were still sinners, Christ died for us. Now that we have been justified by his blood, it is all the more certain that we shall be saved by him from God's wrath. For if, when we were God's enemies, we were reconciled to him by the death of his Son, it is all the more certain that we who have been reconciled will be saved by his life. Not only that; we go so far as to make God our boast through our Lord Jesus Christ, through whom we have now received reconciliation.

K. Isaiah 53:1-12 *An Old Testament Prediction of the Savior's Sufferings*

Who would believe what we have heard?
   To whom has the arm of the LORD been revealed?
He grew up like a sapling before him,
   like a shoot from the parched earth;
There was in him no stately bearing to make us look
    at him,
   nor appearance that would attract us to him.
He was spurned and avoided by men,
   a man of suffering, accustomed to infirmity,
One of those from whom men hide their faces,
   spurned, and we held him in no esteem.

Yet it was our infirmities that he bore.
   our sufferings that he endured,
While we thought of him as stricken,
   as one smitten by God and afflicted.
But he was pierced for our offenses,
   crushed for our sins;
Upon him was the chastisement that makes us whole,
   by his stripes we were healed.
We had all gone astray like sheep,
   each following his own way;
But the LORD laid upon him the guilt of us all.

Though he was harshly treated, he submitted
   and opened not his mouth;
Like a lamb led to the slaughter
   or a sheep before the shearers,
   he was silent and opened not his mouth.
Oppressed and condemned, he was taken away,
   and who would have thought any more of his
      destiny?
When he was cut off from the land of the living,
   and smitten for the sin of his people,
A grave was assigned him among the wicked
   and a burial place with evildoers,
Though he had done no wrong, nor spoken any
      falsehood.
[But the LORD was pleased to crush him in infirmity.]

If he gives his life as an offering for sin,
   he shall see his descendants in a long life,
and the will of the LORD shall be accomplished
      through him.

Because of his affliction he shall see the light in
      fullness of days;
Through his suffering, my servant shall justify many,
   and their guilt he shall bear.
Therefore I will give him his portion among the great,
   and he shall divide the spoils with the mighty,
Because he surrendered himself to death
   and was counted among the wicked;
And he shall take away the sins of many,
   and win pardon for their offenses.

L. Ezekiel 18:20-32 *The Converted Sinner Shall Live*

Only the one who sins shall die. The son shall not be
charged with the guilt of his father, nor shall the
father be charged with the guilt of his son. The
virtuous man's virtue shall be his own, as the wicked

23

man's wickedness shall be his.

But if the wicked man turns away from all the sins he committed, if he keeps all my statutes and does what is right and just, he shall surely live, he shall not die. None of the crimes he committed shall be remembered against him; he shall live because of the virtue he has practiced. Do I indeed derive any pleasure from the death of the wicked? says the Lord GOD. Do I not rather rejoice when he turns from his evil way that he may live?

And if the virtuous man turns from the path of virtue to do evil, the same kind of abominable things that the wicked man does, can he do this and still live? None of his virtuous deeds shall be remembered, because he has broken faith and committed sin; because of this, he shall die. You say, "The LORD's way is not fair!" Hear now, house of Israel: Is it my way that is unfair, or rather, are not your ways unfair? When a virtuous man turns away from virtue to commit iniquity, and dies, it is because of the iniquity he committed that he must die. But if a wicked man, turning from the wickedness he has committed, does what is right and just, he shall preserve his life; since he has turned away from all the sins which he committed, he shall surely live, he shall not die. And yet the house of Israel says, "The LORD's way is not fair!" Is it my way that is not fair, house of Israel, or rather, is it not that your ways are not fair?

Therefore I will judge you, house of Israel, each one according to his ways, says the Lord GOD. Turn and be converted from all your crimes, that they may be no cause of guilt for you. Cast away from you all the crimes you have committed, and make for yourselves a new heart and a new spirit. Why should you die, O house of Israel? For I have no pleasure in the death of anyone who dies, says the Lord GOD. Return and live!

M. Daniel 9:4-23 *The Confession of Daniel*

I prayed to the LORD, my God, and confessed,
"Ah, LORD, great and awesome God, you who keep
your merciful covenant toward those who love you
and observe your commandments! We have sinned,
been wicked and done evil; we have rebelled and
departed from your commandments and your laws.
We have not obeyed your servants the prophets, who
spoke in your name to our kings, our princes, our
fathers, and all the people of the land.
Justice, O Lord, is on your side; we are shamefaced
even to this day; the men of Judah, the residents of
Jerusalem, and all Israel, near and far, in all the
countries to which you have scattered them because
of their treachery toward you. O LORD, we are
shamefaced, like our kings, our princes, and our fathers,
for having sinned against you. But yours, O Lord, our
God, are compassion and forgiveness! Yet we rebelled
against you and paid no heed to your command,
O LORD, our God, to live by the law you gave us
through your servants the prophets. Because all Israel
transgressed your law and went astray, not heeding
your voice, the sworn malediction, recorded in the
law of Moses, the servant of God, was poured out over
us for our sins. You carried out the threats you spoke
against us and against those who governed us, by
bringing upon us in Jerusalem the greatest calamity
that has ever occurred under heaven. As it is written in
the law of Moses, this calamity came full upon us. As
we did not appease the LORD, our God, by turning
back from our wickedness and recognizing his
constancy, so the LORD kept watch over the calamity
and brought it upon us. You, O LORD, our God, are
just in all that you have done, for we did not listen to
your voice.
      "Now, O Lord, our God, who led your people out

of the land of Egypt with a strong hand, and made a
name for yourself even to this day, we have sinned,
we are guilty. O Lord, in keeping with all your just
deeds, let your anger and your wrath be turned away
from your city Jerusalem, your holy mountain. On
account of our sins and the crimes of our fathers,
Jerusalem and your people have become the reproach
of all our neighbors. Hear, therefore, O God, the
prayer and petition of your servant; and for your own
sake, O Lord, let your face shine upon your desolate
sanctuary. Give ear, O my God, and listen; open your
eyes and see our ruins and the city which bears your
name. When we present our petition before you, we
rely not on our just deeds, but on your great mercy.
O Lord, hear! O Lord, pardon! O Lord, be attentive
and act without delay, for your own sake, O my God,
because this city and your people bear your name!"

I was still occupied with my prayer, confessing my
sin and the sin of my people Israel, presenting my
petition to the LORD, my God, on behalf of his holy
mountain—I was still occupied with this prayer, when
Gabriel, the one whom I had seen before in vision,
came to me in rapid flight at the time of the evening
sacrifice. He instructed me in these words: "Daniel, I
have now come to give you understanding. When
you began your petition, an answer was given which I
have come to announce, because you are beloved.
Therefore, mark the answer and understand the
vision."

N. Isaiah 55:1-12 *The Mysterious Ways and
Mercy of God*

All you who are thirsty,
  come to the water!
You who have no money,

come, receive grain and eat;
Come, without paying and without cost,
    drink wine and milk!
Why spend your money for what is not bread;
    your wages for what fails to satisfy?
Heed me, and you shall eat well,
    you shall delight in rich fare.
Come to me heedfully,
    listen, that you may have life.
I will renew with you the everlasting covenant,
    the benefits assured to David.
As I made him a witness to the peoples,
    a leader and commander of nations,
So shall you summon a nation you knew not,
    and nations that knew you not shall run to you,
Because of the Lord, your God,
    the Holy One of Israel, who has glorified you.

Seek the LORD while he may be found,
    call him while he is near.
Let the scoundrel forsake his way,
    and the wicked man his thoughts;
Let him turn to the LORD for mercy;
    to our God, who is generous in forgiving.
For my thoughts are not your thoughts,
    nor are your ways my ways, says the LORD.
As high as the heavens are above the earth,
    so high are my ways above your ways
    and my thoughts above your thoughts.

For just as from the heavens
    the rain and snow come down
And do not return there
    till they have watered the earth,
    making it fertile and fruitful,
Giving seed to him who sows
    and bread to him who eats,

So shall my word be
   that goes forth from my mouth;
It shall not return to me void,
   but shall do my will,
   achieving the end for which I sent it.
Yes, in joy you shall depart,
   in peace you shall be brought back;
Mountains and hills shall break out in song before you,
   and all the trees of the countryside shall clap their
      hands.

O. Ezekiel 34:11-16 *God Is the Good Shepherd*

For thus says the Lord GOD: I myself will look
after and tend my sheep. As a shepherd tends his
flock when he finds himself among his scattered sheep,
so will I tend my sheep. I will rescue them from
every place where they were scattered when it was
cloudy and dark. I will lead them out from among the
peoples and gather them from the foreign lands; I will
bring them back to their own country and pasture
them upon the mountains of Israel [in the land's
ravines and all its inhabited places]. In good pastures
will I pasture them, and on the mountain heights of
Israel shall be their grazing ground. There they shall
lie down on good grazing ground, and in rich pastures
shall they be pastured on the mountains of Israel. I
myself will pasture my sheep; I myself will give them
rest, says the Lord GOD. The lost I will seek out, the
strayed I will bring back, the injured I will bind up,
the sick I will heal [but the sleek and the strong I will
destroy], shepherding them rightly.

P. Joel 2:12-19 *A Call to Repent*

Yet even now, says the LORD,
   return to me with your whole heart,

with fasting, and weeping, and mourning;
Rend your hearts, not your garments,
    and return to the LORD, your God.
For gracious and merciful is he,
    slow to anger, rich in kindness,
    and relenting in punishment.
Perhaps he will again relent
    and leave behind him a blessing,
Offerings and libations
    for the LORD, your God.

Blow the trumpet in Zion!
    proclaim a fast,
    call an assembly;
Gather the people,
    notify the congregation;
Assemble the elders,
    gather the children
    and the infants at the breast;
Let the bridegroom quit his room,
    and the bride her chamber.
Between the porch and the altar
    let the priests, the ministers of the LORD, weep,
And say, "Spare, O Lord, your people,
    and make not your heritage a reproach,
    with the nations ruling over them!
Why should they say among the peoples,
    'Where is their God?' "

Then the Lord was stirred to concern for his land and
took pity on his people. The Lord answered and said to
his people:

See, I will send you grain, and wine, and oil
    and you shall be filled with them;
No more will I make you
    a reproach among the nations.

Q. Micah 7:2-7, 18-20 *Confidence in God's Mercy*

The faithful are gone from the earth,
    among men the upright are no more!
They all lie in wait to shed blood,
    each one ensnares the other.
Their hands succeed at evil;
    the prince makes demands,
The judge is had for a price,
    The great man speaks as he pleases,
The best of them is like a brier,
    the most upright like a thorn hedge.
The day announced by your watchmen!
    your punishment has come;
    now is the time of your confusion.
Put no trust in a friend,
    have no confidence in a companion;
Against her who lies in your bosom
    guard the portals of your mouth.
For the son dishonors his father,
    the daughter rises up against her mother,
The daughter-in-law against her mother-in-law,
    and a man's enemies are those of his household.
But as for me, I will look to the Lord,
    I will put my trust in God my savior;
    my God will hear me!

Who is there like you, the God who removes guilt
    and pardons sin for the remnant of his inheritance;
Who does not persist in anger forever,
    but delights rather in clemency,
And will again have compassion on us,
    treading underfoot our guilt?
You will cast into the depths of the sea
    all our sins;
You will show faithfulness to Jacob,
    and grace to Abraham,
As you have sworn to our fathers
    from days of old.

Step 3:
A Look Into the Heart

This step requires a period of reflection sufficient for you to look at the past (How long since you last received the sacrament?) and to search out your sins over that period.

Are there sins because of what you did or what you failed to do? What sinful failures can you recall in thought, word or deed?

Serious sins, i.e., major wrongs committed or omitted with full awareness and total freedom, will probably come quickly to your attention or already press heavily on your mind.

These should be confessed in this way: what you did (or failed to do), any major circumstances which notably change the kind of sin it was, and the approximate number of times.

Lesser sins need not be confessed. However, they are moral failures, too, and can be forgiven in the sacrament of Penance. Frankly confessing a few of them can help you conquer those faults and grow into the kind of person God wants you to become.

This reflective look at the past should be honest, down to earth, painful, but healthy and healing. Don't spend too long or dig too deeply; yet don't play games either or avoid coming to grips with what you know was wrong in the past.

A contemporary psychiatrist has this to say: "So long as a person lives under the shadow of real, unacknowledged, and unexpiated guilt, he . . . will continue to hate himself and to suffer the inevitable consequences of self-hatred. But the moment he . . . begins to accept his guilt and his sinfulness, the possibility of radical reformation opens up; and . . . a new freedom of self-respect and peace."[1]

If you would like some assistance here, the suggestions below may open up a few avenues of thought and lead to a better appreciation of what Jesus demands from his followers.

A. The Law of Love:

One of the scribes came up, and when he heard them arguing he realized how skillfully Jesus answered them. He decided to ask him, "Which is the first of all the commandments?" Jesus replied: "This is the first:

'Hear, O Israel! The Lord our God is Lord alone! Therefore you shall love the Lord your God
   with all your heart,
   with all your soul,
   with all your mind,
   and with all your strength.'
This is the second,
   'You shall love your neighbor as yourself.'
There is no other commandment greater than these." The scribe said to him: "Excellent, Teacher! You are right in saying, 'He is the One, there is no other than he.' Yes, 'to love him with all our heart, with all our thoughts and with all our strength, and to love our neighbor as ourselves' is worth more than any burnt offering or sacrifice." Jesus approved the insight of this answer and told him, "You are not far from the reign of God." And no one had the courage to ask him any more questions.—Mark 12:28-34

---

1. O. Hobart Mowrer, quoted in Karl Menninger's *Whatever Became of Sin?* Hawthorn Books, New York, 1973, p. 195.

Sin could well be spelled with a capital "I" in the middle. Sinful behavior is essentially selfish behavior. Sinners basically choose in a harmful, aggressive way the "I" over the "You" or seek someone, perhaps something, which is in fact self-destructive.

Love, on the contrary, is in its essence unselfish and self-giving.

Jesus' words to the scribe, then, present his followers with a simple, yet extremely taxing and personal guide for their lives.

That law of love taxes in an ongoing manner all our resources since it forms an ideal we never can reach, but merely strive to fulfill.

This commandment of Christ also takes on a highly personal character. Only I can judge if what I did or failed to do was selfish or not; and in some circumstances I am not even sure myself about the motivation behind certain actions or omissions.

The questions we ask at this point: Have I been selfish with regard to others? Have I chosen what I wanted, not what was best for me, and thus ultimately hurt myself in the process?

B. A Call to Holiness:

"In a word, you must be perfect as your heavenly Father is perfect." (Matthew 5:48)

If it has been many months or a few years since you last confessed your sins and you cannot think of anything at all to confess, this may be the moment to reflect on those words of Christ. Our Lord calls us to lead holy, perfect lives. If we have not seriously failed God, our neighbor or ourself, we could say wonderful, praise the Lord. But that is only a beginning step. Eliminating lesser sins, overcoming imperfections and putting on virtues detailed for us in the New Testament require a lifelong, uneven, often discouraging struggle. The victories and defeats in that effort are good subject matter for confession.

The story of a good man summoned by Jesus to become a better, perfect one follows.

As he was setting out on a journey a man came running up, knelt down before him and asked, "Good Teacher, what must I do to share in everlasting life?" Jesus answered, "Why do you call me good? No one is good but God alone. You know the commandments:
'You shall not kill;
You shall not commit adultery;
You shall not steal;
You shall not bear false witness;
You shall not defraud;
Honor your father and your mother.' "

He replied, "Teacher, I have kept all these since my childhood." Then Jesus looked at him with love and told him, "There is one thing more you must do. Go and sell what you have and give to the poor; you will then have treasure in heaven. After that, come and follow me." At these words the man's face fell. He went away sad, for he had many possessions. Jesus looked around and said to his disciples, "How hard it is for the rich to enter the kingdom of God!" The disciples could only marvel at his words. So Jesus repeated what he had said: "My sons, how hard it is to enter the kingdom of God! It is easier for a camel to pass through a needle's eye than for a rich man to enter the kingdom of God."

They were completely overwhelmed at this, and exclaimed to one another, "Then who can be saved?"
—Mark 10:17-26

C. Triple Effects of Sin:

Sin destroys or weakens our friendship with God, ruins or hinders our relationships with others, and upsets the beauty or harmony of the world around us.

To repent, to change our hearts and ways involves a healing of these three wounds. We need to be reconciled with the Lord, with our neighbor and with the environment.

The book of Genesis, in its classic, poetic account of man's fall, describes those triple effects of sin: Adam and Eve lost God's special friendship, found their mutual relationships impaired (he blamed her; one of their children murdered the other), and witnessed the destruction of nature's peaceful pattern.

Now the serpent was the most cunning of all the animals that the LORD God had made. The serpent asked the woman, "Did God really tell you not to eat from any of the trees in the garden?" The woman answered the serpent: "We may eat of the fruit of the trees in the garden; it is only about the fruit of the tree in the middle of the garden that God said, 'You shall not eat it or even touch it, lest you die.'" But the serpent said to the woman: "You certainly will not die! No, God knows well that the moment you eat of it your eyes will be opened and you will be like gods who know what is good and what is bad." The woman saw that the tree was good for food, pleasing to the eyes, and desirable for gaining wisdom. So she took some of its fruit and ate it; and she also gave some to her husband, who was with her, and he ate it. Then the eyes of both of them were opened, and they realized that they were naked; so they sewed fig leaves together and made loincloths for themselves.

When they heard the sound of the LORD God moving about in the garden at the breezy time of the day, the man and his wife hid themselves from the LORD God among the trees of the garden. The LORD God then called to the man and asked him, "Where are you?" He answered, "I heard you in the garden;

35

but I was afraid, because I was naked, so I hid myself."
Then he asked, "Who told you that you were naked?
You have eaten, then, from the tree of which I had
forbidden you to eat!" The man replied, "The
woman whom you put here with me—she gave me
fruit from the tree, and so I ate it." The LORD God
then asked the woman, "Why did you do such a
thing?" The woman answered, "The serpent tricked
me into it, so I ate it."
    Then the LORD God said to the serpent:

"Because you have done this, you shall be banned
    from all the animals
    and from all the wild creatures;
On your belly shall you crawl
    and dirt shall you eat
    all the days of your life.
I will put enmity between you and the woman,
    and between your offspring and hers;
He will strike at your head,
    while you strike at his heel."

To the woman he said:
"I will intensify the pangs of your childbearing;
    in pain shall you bring forth children.
Yet your urge shall be for your husband,
    and he shall be your master."

To the man he said: "Because you listened to your
wife and ate from the tree of which I had forbidden
you to eat,

    "Cursed be the ground because of you!
In toil shall you eat its yield all the days of your life.
Thorns and thistles shall it bring forth to you,
    as you eat of the plants of the field.
By the sweat of your face

shall you get bread to eat,
Until you return to the ground,
    from which you were taken;
For you are dirt,
    and to dirt you shall return."—Genesis 3:1-19

The man had relations with his wife Eve, and she
conceived and bore Cain, saying, "I have produced
a man with the help of the LORD." Next she bore
his brother Abel. Abel became a keeper of flocks, and
Cain a tiller of the soil. In the course of time Cain
brought an offering to the LORD from the fruit of the
soil, while Abel, for his part, brought one of the best
firstlings of his flock. The LORD looked with favor
on Abel and his offering, but on Cain and his offering
he did not. Cain greatly resented this and was crestfallen. So the LORD said to Cain: "Why are you so
resentful and crestfallen? If you do well, you can hold
up your head; but if not, sin is a demon lurking at
the door: his urge is toward you, yet you can be
his master."
    Cain said to his brother Abel, "Let us go out in
the field." When they were in the field, Cain attacked
his brother Abel and killed him. Then the LORD
asked Cain, "Where is your brother Abel?" He answered, "I do not know. Am I my brother's keeper?"
The LORD then said: "What have you done! Listen:
your brother's blood cries out to me from the soil!
Therefore you shall be banned from the soil that
opened its mouth to receive your brother's blood from
your hand. If you till the soil, it shall no longer give
you its produce. You shall become a restless wanderer
on the earth." Cain said to the LORD: "My punishment is too great to bear. Since you have now
banished me from the soil, and I must avoid your
presence and become a restless wanderer on the
earth, anyone may kill me at sight." "Not so!" the

37

LORD said to him. "If anyone kills Cain, Cain shall be avenged sevenfold." So the LORD put a mark on Cain, lest anyone should kill him at sight.
—Genesis 4:1-15

D. The Bare Minimum:

The ten commandments give us good guidelines for our lives. There would be peace on earth, if every person kept these divine rules. Yet the Christian is summoned higher and asked to move beyond those laws.

They form, then, a kind of bare minimum. If we have violated them, we know our lives have slipped below the danger point and certainly cannot call ourselves good Christians. That title is reserved for those who keep these precepts which follow *and* faithfully pursue the course Jesus sketched for us by his life and teaching.

Then God delivered all these commandments:
"I, the LORD, am your God, who brought you out of the land of Egypt, that place of slavery. You shall not have other gods besides me. You shall not carve idols for yourselves in the shape of anything in the sky above or on the earth below or in the waters beneath the earth; you shall not bow down before them or worship them. For I, the LORD, your God, am a jealous God, inflicting punishment for their fathers' wickedness on the children of those who hate me, down to the third and fourth generation; but bestowing mercy down to the thousandth generation, on the children of those who love me and keep my commandments.

"You shall not take the name of the LORD, your God, in vain. For the LORD will not leave unpunished him who takes his name in vain.

"Remember to keep holy the sabbath day. Six days you may labor and do all your work, but the seventh day is the sabbath of the LORD, your God. No work may be done then either by you, or your son or daughter, or your male or female slave, or your beast, or by the alien who lives with you. In six days the LORD made the heavens and the earth, the sea and all that is in them; but on the seventh day he rested. That is why the LORD has blessed the sabbath day and made it holy.

"Honor your father and your mother, that you may have a long life in the land which the LORD, your God, is giving you.

"You shall not kill.

"You shall not commit adultery.

"You shall not steal.

"You shall not bear false witness against your neighbor.

"You shall not covet your neighbor's house. You shall not covet your neighbor's wife, nor his male or female slave, nor his ox or ass, nor anything else that belongs to him."

When the people witnessed the thunder and lightning, the trumpet blast and the mountain smoking, they all feared and trembled. So they took up a position much farther away and said to Moses, "You speak to us, and we will listen; but let not God speak to us, or we shall die." Moses answered the people, "Do not be afraid, for God has come to you only to test you and put his fear upon you, lest you should sin." Still the people remained at a distance, while Moses approached the cloud where God was.—Exodus 20:1-21

E. Service or Neglect of Those in Need:

The description of the last judgment which follows can both reassure our hearts and, at the same time, leave us uneasy. It preaches that God remembers those occasions when we recognized Christ in our needy neighbor and responded accordingly; it also teaches that the Lord recalls those situations when we failed to see Jesus in troubled persons and neglected them.

Unfortunately few, if any of us, can come up with a perfect score on this test. Think of several particularly difficult cases—the confused patient in a nursing home, the emotionally or mentally disturbed, the deeply rebellious youngster, the "con" artist who seeks a handout, the constantly imposing neighbor or relative, the alcoholic, the unpleasant personnel at work— and judge yourself according to the gospel standards.

"When the Son of Man comes in his glory, escorted by all the angels of heaven, he will sit upon his royal throne, and all the nations will be assembled before him. Then he will separate them into two groups, as a shepherd separates sheep from goats. The sheep he will place on his right hand, the goats on his left. The king will say to those on his right: 'Come. You have my Father's blessing! Inherit the kingdom prepared for you from the creation of the world. For I was hungry and you gave me food, I was thirsty and you gave me drink. I was a stranger and you welcomed me, naked and you clothed me. I was ill and you comforted me, in prison and you came to visit me.' Then the just will ask him: 'Lord, when did we see you hungry and feed you or see you thirsty and give you drink? When did we welcome you away from home or clothe you in your nakedness? When did we visit you when you were ill or in prison?' The king will answer them: 'I assure you, as often as you did it for one of my least brothers, you did it for me.'

"Then he will say to those on his left: 'Out of my sight, you condemned, into that everlasting fire prepared for the devil and his angels! I was hungry and you gave me no food, I was thirsty and you gave me no drink. I was away from home and you gave me no welcome, naked and you gave me no clothing. I was ill and in prison and you did not come to comfort me.' Then they in turn will ask: 'Lord, when did we see you hungry or thirsty or away from home or naked, or ill or in prison and not attend you in your needs?' He will answer them: 'I assure you, as often as you neglected to do it to one of these least ones, you neglected to do it to me.' These will go off to eternal punishment and the just to eternal life."
—Matthew 25:31-46

F. Misusing Ourselves and Others:

St. Paul in several places takes the ideal law of love and applies it to very specific circumstances.

My brothers, remember that you have been called to live in freedom—but not a freedom that gives free rein to the flesh. Out of love, place yourselves at one another's service. The whole law has found its fulfillment in this one saying: "You shall love your neighbor as yourself." If you go on biting and tearing one another to pieces, take care! You will end up in mutual destruction!

My point is that you should live in accord with the spirit and you will not yield to the cravings of the flesh. The flesh lusts against the spirit and the spirit against the flesh; the two are directly opposed. This is why you do not do what your will intends. If you are guided by the spirit, you are not under the law. It is obvious what proceeds from the flesh: lewd

41

conduct, impurity, licentiousness, idolatry, sorcery, hostilities, bickering, jealousy, outbursts of rage, selfish rivalries, dissensions, factions, envy, drunkenness, orgies, and the like. I warn you, as I have warned you before: those who do such things will not inherit the kingdom of God!

In contrast, the fruit of the spirit is love, joy, peace, patient endurance, kindness, generosity, faith, mildness, and chastity. Against such there is no law! Those who belong to Christ Jesus have crucified their flesh with its passions and desires. Since we live by the spirit, let us follow the spirit's lead. Let us never be boastful, or challenging, or jealous toward one another.—Galatians 5:13-26

Be imitators of God as his dear children. Follow the way of love, even as Christ loved you. He gave himself for us as an offering to God, a gift of pleasing fragrance.

As for lewd conduct or promiscuousness or lust of any sort, let them not even be mentioned among you; your holiness forbids this. Nor should there be any obscene, silly, or suggestive talk; all that is out of place. Instead, give thanks. Make no mistake about this: no fornicator, no unclean or lustful person—in effect an idolater—has any inheritance in the kingdom of Christ and of God. Let no one deceive you with worthless arguments. These are sins that bring God's wrath down on the disobedient; therefore have nothing to do with them.

There was a time when you were darkness, but now you are light in the Lord. Well, then, live as children of light. Light produces every kind of goodness and justice and truth. Be correct in your judgment of what pleases the Lord. Take no part in vain deeds done in darkness; rather, condemn them. It is shameful even to mention the things these people do in secret; but when such deeds are condemned they are seen in the light of day, and all that then appears is light. That is why we read:

> "Awake, O sleeper,
>   arise from the dead,
>   and Christ will give you light."

Keep careful watch over your conduct. Do not act like fools, but like thoughtful men. Make the most of the present opportunity, for these are evil days. Do not continue in ignorance, but try to discern the will of the Lord. Avoid getting drunk on wine; that leads to debauchery. Be filled with the Spirit, addressing one another in psalms and hymns and inspired songs. Sing praise to the Lord with all your hearts. Give thanks to God the Father always and for everything in the name of our Lord Jesus Christ.—Ephesians 5:1-20

G. Forgiveness of Others:

If you have been hurt by someone, are nursing a grudge, just can't forgive, much less forget an offense, harbor resentment or seek revenge, then God's words below may say something to you.

Then Peter came up and asked him, "Lord, when my brother wrongs me, how often must I forgive him? Seven times?" "No," Jesus replied, "not seven times; I say, seventy times seven times. That is why the reign of God may be said to be like a king who decided to settle accounts with his officials. When he began his auditing, one was brought in who owed him a huge amount. As he had no way of paying it, his master ordered him to be sold, along with his wife, his children, and all his property, in payment of the debt. At that the official prostrated himself in homage and said, 'My lord, be patient with me and I will pay you back in full.' Moved with pity, the master let the official go and wrote off the debt. But when that same official went out he met a fellow servant who owed him a mere fraction of what he himself owed. He seized him and throttled him. 'Pay back what you owe,' he demanded. His fellow servant dropped to his knees and began to plead with him, 'Just give me time and I will pay you back in full.' But he would hear none of it. Instead, he had him put in jail until he paid back what he owed. When his fellow servants saw what had happened they were badly shaken, and went to their master to report the whole incident. His master sent for him and said, 'You worthless wretch! I canceled your entire debt when you pleaded with me. Should you not have dealt mercifully with your fellow servant, as I dealt with you?" Then in anger the master handed him over to the torturers until he paid back all that he owed. My heavenly Father will treat you in exactly the same way unless each of you forgives his brother from his heart."—Matthew 18:21-35

"You have heard the commandment imposed on your forefathers, 'You shall not commit murder; every murderer shall be liable to judgment.' What I say to you is: everyone who grows angry with his brother shall be liable to judgment; any man who uses abusive language toward his brother shall be answerable to the Sanhedrin, and if he holds him in contempt he risks the fires of Gehenna. If you bring your gift to the altar and there recall that your brother has anything against you, leave your gift at the altar, go first to be reconciled with your brother, and then come and offer your gift. Lose no time; settle with your opponent while on your way to court with him. Otherwise your opponent may hand you over to the guard, who will throw you into prison. I warn you, you will not be released until you have paid the last penny."—Matthew 5:21-26

"You have heard the commandment, 'An eye for an eye, a tooth for a tooth.' But what I say to you is: offer no resistance to injury. When a person strikes you on the right cheek, turn and offer him the other. If anyone wants to go to law over your shirt, hand him your coat as well. Should anyone press you into service for one mile, go with him two miles. Give to the man who begs from you. Do not turn your back on the borrower.

"You have heard the commandment, 'You shall love your countryman but hate your enemy.' My command to you is: love your enemies, pray for your persecutors. This will prove that you are sons of your heavenly Father, for his sun rises on the bad and the good, he rains on the just and the unjust. If you love those who love you, what merit is there in that? Do not tax collectors do as much? And if you greet your brothers only, what is so praiseworthy about that? Do not pagans do as much?"—Matthew 5:38-47

"If you forgive the faults of others, your heavenly Father will forgive you yours. If you do not forgive others, neither will your Father forgive you."—Matthew 6:14-15

There will be no true or deep peace in our hearts until we are willing to forgive those who have injured us.

H. A Call to Prayer:

The bible offers several principles to guide us in our prayer life as Christians.

Pray frequently:

Finally, draw your strength from the Lord and his mighty power. Put on the armor of God so that you may be able to stand firm against the tactics of the devil. Our battle is not against human forces but against the principalities and powers, the rulers of this world of darkness, the evil spirits in regions above. You must put on the armor of God if you are to resist on the evil day; do all that your duty requires, and hold your ground. Stand fast, with the truth as the belt around your waist, justice as your breastplate, and zeal to propagate the gospel of peace as your footgear. In all circumstances hold faith up before you as your shield; it will help you extinguish the fiery darts of the evil one. Take the helmet of salvation and the sword of the spirit, the word of God.

At every opportunity pray in the Spirit, using prayers and petitions of every sort. Pray constantly and at-tentively for all in the holy company.—Ephesians 6:10-18

Pray from a pure heart for the proper reason:

"Be on guard against performing religious acts for people to see. Otherwise expect no recompense from your heavenly Father. . . . When you are praying, do not behave like the hypocrites who love to stand and pray in synagogues or on street corners in order to be noticed. I give you my word, they are already repaid. Whenever you pray, go to your room, close

your door, and pray to your Father in private. Then your Father, who sees what no man sees, will repay you. In your prayer do not rattle on like the pagans. They think they will win a hearing by the sheer multiplication of words. Do not imitate them. Your Father knows what you need before you ask him."
—Matthew 6:1, 5-8

Pray together with others:

"Again I tell you, if two of you join your voices on earth to pray for anything whatever, it shall be granted you by my Father in heaven. Where two or three are gathered in my name, there am I in their midst."—Matthew 18:19-20

Pray with persistence and confidence:

One day he was praying in a certain place. When he had finished, one of his disciples asked him, "Lord, teach us to pray, as John taught his disciples." He said to them, "When you pray, say:
   "Father,
   hallowed be your name,
   your kingdom come.
   Give us each day our daily bread.
   Forgive us our sins
   for we too forgive all who do us wrong;
   and subject us not to the trial."
Jesus said to them: "If one of you knows someone who comes to him in the middle of the night and says to him, 'Friend, lend me three loaves, for a friend of mine has come in from a journey and I have nothing to offer him'; and he from inside should reply, 'Leave me alone. The door is shut now and my children and I are in bed. I cannot get up to look after your needs'—I tell you, even though he does not get up

and take care of the man because of friendship, he will do so because of his persistence, and give him as much as he needs.

"So I say to you, 'Ask and you shall receive; seek and you shall find; knock and it shall be opened to you.'

"For whoever asks, receives; whoever seeks, finds; whoever knocks, is admitted. What father among you will give his son a snake if he asks for a fish, or hand him a scorpion if he asks for an egg? If you, with all your sins, know how to give your children good things, how much more will the heavenly Father give the Holy Spirit to those who ask him."
—Luke 11:1-13

How would you evaluate yourself in this area according to these principles?

I. Self-righteously Passing Judgments:

If you really think you are better than someone else, tend to be patronizing, look down on others, quickly judge people or speak unkindly about them, the passages which follow should prove of interest.

"If you want to avoid judgment, stop passing judgment. Your verdict on others will be the verdict passed on you. The measure with which you measure will be used to measure you. Why look at the speck in your brother's eye when you miss the plank in your own? How can you say to your brother, 'Let me take that speck out of your eye,' while all the time the plank remains in your own? You hypocrite! Remove the plank from your own eye first; then you will see clearly to take the speck from your brother's eye."
—Matthew 7:1-5

He then spoke this parable addressed to those who believed in their own self-righteousness while holding everyone else in contempt: "Two men went up to the temple to pray; one was a Pharisee, the other a tax collector. The Pharisee with head unbowed prayed in this fashion: 'I give you thanks, O God, that I am not like the rest of men—grasping, crooked, adulterous—or even like this tax collector. I fast twice a week. I pay tithes on all I possess.' The other man, however, kept his distance, not even daring to raise his eyes to heaven. All he did was beat his breast and say, 'O God, be merciful to me, a sinner.' Believe me, this man went home from the temple justified but the other did not. For everyone who exalts himself shall be humbled while he who humbles himself shall be exalted."—Luke 18:9-14

In the name of the encouragement you owe me in Christ, in the name of the solace that love can give, of fellowship in spirit, compassion, and pity, I beg you: make my joy complete by your unanimity, possessing the one love, united in spirit and ideals. Never act out of rivalry or conceit; rather, let all parties think humbly of others as superior to themselves, each of you looking to others' interests rather than to his own.—Philippians 2:1-4

Not many of you should become teachers, my brothers; you should realize that those of us who do so will be called to the stricter account. All of us fall short in many respects. If a person is without fault in speech he is a man in the fullest sense, because he can control his entire body. When we put bits into the mouths of horses to make them obey us, we guide the rest of their bodies. It is the same with ships: however large they are, and despite the fact that they are driven by fierce winds, they are directed

49

by very small rudders on whatever course the steersman's impulse may select. The tongue is something like that. It is a small member, yet it makes great pretensions.

See how tiny the spark is that sets a huge forest ablaze! The tongue is such a flame. It exists among our members as a whole universe of malice. The tongue defiles the entire body. Its flames encircle our course from birth, and its fire is kindled by hell. Every form of life, four-footed or winged, crawling or swimming, can be tamed, and has been tamed, by mankind; the tongue no man can tame. It is a restless evil, full of deadly poison. We use it to say, "Praised be the Lord and Father"; then we use it to curse men, though they are made in the likeness of God. Blessing and curse come out of the same mouth. This ought not to be, my brothers! Does a spring gush forth fresh water and foul from the same outlet? A fig tree, brothers, cannot produce olives, or a grapevine figs; no more can a brackish source yield fresh water.
—James 3:1-12

J. Fidelity in Marriage:

Have you been loyal and true to your partner in good times and in bad, in sickness and in health, when rich and when poor, at 46 as well as 21? There should be no double standard here—a set of strict rules for the wife and a more relaxed code for the husband. Christian teaching demands faithfulness in thought and word, as well as deed.

"You have heard the commandment, 'You shall not commit adultery.' What I say to you is: anyone who looks lustfully at a woman has already committed adultery with her in his thoughts. If your right eye is

your trouble, gouge it out and throw it away! Better
to lose part of your body than to have it all cast into
Gehenna. Again, if your right hand is your trouble
cut it off and throw it away! Better to lose part of
your body than to have it all cast into Gehenna.

It was also said, 'Whenever a man divorces his wife,
he must give her a decree of divorce.' What I say to
you is: everyone who divorces his wife—lewd conduct is a separate case—forces her to commit adultery.
The man who marries a divorced woman likewise
commits adultery."—Matthew 5:27-32

K. Correcting Another:

Few find this a pleasant task. We often run away
from the duty or prefer to withdraw in silence, then
grumble to ourselves or complain to others. Fraternal
correction takes courage, requires pure motives, pre-
supposes sensitivity and does not always succeed. Jesus
urges a few steps in the process.

"If your brother should commit some wrong against
you, go and point out his fault, but keep it between
the two of you. If he listens to you, you have won
your brother over. If he does not listen, summon
another, so that every case may stand on the word of
two or three witnesses. If he ignores them, refer it
to the church. If he ignores even the church, then
treat him as you would a Gentile or a tax collector."
I assure you, whatever you declare bound on earth
shall be held bound in heaven, and whatever you
declare loosed on earth shall be held loosed in heaven.
—Matthew 18:15-18

L. True Riches and Trust in God:

Are you worrying too much and not trusting enough? Overly ambitious? Excessively concerned about money? Unwilling to share what you possess with others?

"Do not lay up for yourselves an earthly treasure. Moths and rust corrode; thieves break in and steal. Make it your practice instead to store up heavenly treasure, which neither moths nor rust corrode nor thieves break in and steal. Remember, where your treasure is, there your heart is also. The eye is the body's lamp. If your eyes are good, your body will be filled with light; if your eyes are bad, your body will be in darkness. And if your light is darkness, how deep will the darkness be! No man can serve two masters. He will either hate one and love the other or be attentive to one and despise the other. You cannot give yourself to God and money. I warn you, then: do not worry about your livelihood, what you are to eat or drink or use for clothing. Is not life more than food? Is not the body more valuable than clothes?

"Look at the birds in the sky. They do not sow or reap, they gather nothing into barns; yet your heavenly Father feeds them. Are not you more important than they? Which of you by worrying can add a moment to his life-span? As for clothes, why be concerned? Learn a lesson from the way the wild flowers grow. They do not work; they do not spin. Yet I assure you, not even Solomon in all his splendor was arrayed like one of these. If God can clothe in such splendor the grass of the field, which blooms today and is thrown on the fire tomorrow, will he not provide much more for you, O weak in faith! Stop worrying, then, over questions like, 'What are we to

eat, or what are we to drink, or what are we to wear?'
The unbelievers are always running after these things.
Your heavenly Father knows all that you need. Seek
first his kingship over you, his way of holiness, and
all these things will be given you besides. Enough,
then, of worrying about tomorrow. Let tomorrow
take care of itself. Today has troubles enough of its
own."—Matthew 6:19-34

M. Guidance from the Church:

In connection with the recently revised Rite of
Penance the Congregation of Divine Worship offered
a suggested outline of questions for use in examining
our consciences.*

It first poses three overall inquiries covering certain areas of the past and attitudes about the present.

1. What is my attitude to the sacrament of Penance?
   Do I sincerely want to be set free from sin, to turn
   again to God, to begin a new life, and to enter
   into a deeper friendship with God? Or do I look
   on it as a burden, to be undertaken as seldom as
   possible?

2. Did I forget to mention, or deliberately conceal,
   any grave sins in past confessions?

3. Did I perform the penance I was given? Did I
   make reparation for any injury to others? Have I
   tried to put into practice my resolution to lead a
   better life in keeping with the Gospel?

---

*Rite of Penance. "Appendix III, Form of Examination of Con-
science." Copyright © 1975, International Committee on English in
the Liturgy, Inc. All rights reserved.

53

The "Form of an Examination of Conscience" then presents the penitent with a lengthy list of questions based on God's words which tell us to love the Lord with our whole heart, to love our neighbor as ourself, and to be perfect as our heavenly Father is perfect.

Each individual should examine his life in the light of God's word.

I.

The Lord says: "You shall love the Lord your God with your whole heart."

1. Is my heart set on God, so that I really love him above all things and am faithful to his commandments, as a son loves his father? Or am I more concerned about the things of this world? Have I a right intention in what I do?

2. God spoke to us in his Son: is my faith in God firm and secure? Am I wholehearted in accepting the Church's teaching? Have I been careful to grow in my understanding of the faith, to hear God's word, to listen to instructions on the faith, to avoid dangers to faith? Have I been always strong and fearless in professing my faith in God and the Church? Have I been willing to be known as a Christian in private and public life?

3. Have I prayed morning and evening? When I pray, do I really raise my mind and heart to God or is it a matter of words only? Do I offer God my difficulties, my joys, and my sorrows? Do I turn to God in time of temptation?

4. Have I love and reverence for God's name? Have I offended him in blasphemy, swearing falsely, or taking his name in vain? Have I shown disrespect for the Blessed Virgin Mary and the saints?

5. Do I keep Sundays and feast days holy by taking a full part, with attention and devotion, in the liturgy, and especially in the Mass? Have I fulfilled the precept of annual confession and of communion during the Easter season?

6. Are there false gods that I worship by giving them greater attention and deeper trust than I give to God: money, superstition, spiritism, or other occult practices?

II.

The Lord says: "Love one another as I have loved you."

1. Have I a genuine love for my neighbor? Or do I use them for my own ends, or do to them what I would not want done to myself? Have I given grave scandal by my words or actions?

2. In my family life, have I contributed to the well-being and happiness of the rest of the family by patience and genuine love? Have I been obedient to parents, showing them proper respect and giving them help in their spiritual and material needs? Have I been careful to give a Christian upbringing to my children, and helped them by good example and by exercising authority as a parent? Have I been faithful to my husband (wife), in my heart and in my relations with others?

3. Do I share my possessions with the less fortunate? Do I do my best to help the victims of oppression, misfortune, and poverty? Or do I look down on my neighbor, especially the poor, the sick, the elderly, strangers, and people of other races?

4. Does my life reflect the mission I received in confirmation? Do I share in the apostolic and charitable works of the Church, and in the life of my parish? Have I helped to meet the needs of the Church and of the world, and prayed for them: for unity in the Church, for the spread of the Gospel among the nations, for peace and justice, etc.?

5. Am I concerned for the good and prosperity of the human community in which I live, or do I spend my life caring only for myself? Do I share to the best of my ability in the work of promoting justice, morality, harmony, and love in human relations? Have I done my duty as a citizen? Have I paid my taxes?

6. In my work or profession am I just, hard-working, honest, serving society out of love for others? Have I paid a fair wage to my employees? Have I been faithful to my promises and contracts?

7. Have I obeyed legitimate authority and given it due respect?

8. If I am in a position of responsibility or authority, do I use this for my own advantage or for the good of others, in a spirit of service?

9. Have I been truthful and fair, or have I injured

others by deceit, calumny, detraction, rash judgment, or violation of a secret?

10. Have I done violence to others by damage to life or limb, reputation, honor, or material possessions? Have I involved them in loss? Have I been responsible for advising an abortion or procuring one? Have I kept up hatred for others? Am I estranged from others through quarrels, enmity, insults, anger? Have I been guilty of refusing to testify to the innocence of another because of selfishness?

11. Have I stolen the property of others? Have I desired it unjustly and inordinately? Have I damaged it? Have I made restitution of other people's property and made good their loss?

12. If I have been injured, have I been ready to make peace, for the love of Christ, and to forgive, or do I harbor hatred and the desire for revenge?

III.

Christ our Lord says: "Be perfect as your Father is perfect."

1. Where is my life really leading me? Is the hope of eternal life my inspiration? Have I tried to grow in the life of the Spirit through prayer, reading the word of God and meditating on it, receiving the sacraments, self-denial? Have I been anxious to control my vices, my bad inclinations and passions, e.g., envy, love of food and drink? Have I been proud and boastful, thinking myself better in the sight of God and despising others as less important than myself? Have I imposed my own

will on others, without respecting their freedom and rights?

2. What use have I made of time, of health and strength, of the gifts God has given me to be used like the talents in the Gospel? Do I use them to become more perfect every day? Or have I been lazy and too much given to leisure?

3. Have I been patient in accepting the sorrows and disappointments of life? How have I performed mortification so as to "fill up what is wanting to the sufferings of Christ"? Have I kept the precept of fasting and abstinence?

4. Have I kept my senses and my whole body pure and chaste as a temple of the Holy Spirit consecrated for resurrection and glory, and as a sign of God's faithful love for men and women, a sign that is seen most perfectly in the sacrament of matrimony? Have I dishonored my body by fornication, impurity, unworthy conversation or thoughts, evil desires, or actions? Have I given in to sensuality? Have I indulged in reading, conversation, shows, and entertainments that offend against Christian and human decency? Have I encouraged others to sin by my own failure to maintain these standards? Have I been faithful to the moral law in my married life?

5. Have I gone against my conscience out of fear or hypocrisy?

6. Have I always tried to act in the true freedom of the sons of God according to the law of the Spirit, or am I the slave of forces within me?

Step 4:
The Confession of Sin

The actual confession of sins ideally follows the pattern outlined by the new ritual as indicated below. However, the words you use and the way you say them are of secondary concern. It is the sorrow for sin and the change of heart which really matter.

Should you feel nervous or become forgetful, simply tell the confessor that and ask for his help.

Keep in mind these questions when relating your sins: What did I do? Why did I do it? How can I be better?

At the end of this section you will find two sample confessions which bring out that what, why, how approach.

Some churches provide rooms of reconciliation which offer the opportunity for sit down, face to face confessions as well as for the more customary kneeling behind the screen, anonymous type. When given that choice, simply select the manner you find most comfortable and in which you can confess openly and best find the forgiving peace of Christ.

S
T
E
P
4

Penitents and priests familiar and comfortable with the charismatic view of this sacrament as an occasion for inner healing will find the rite flexible enough to suit that approach. Shared biblical reading, a reflective period seeking the Holy Spirit's guidance, and prayers for healing, deliverance and strengthening can easily be incorporated within its framework.

Regardless of the manner you confess, however, the results should be identical: a sense of forgiveness and freedom, a serenity deep within the heart, a sometimes even conscious awareness of strength received throughout your whole being, a confidence that, reconciled with God, yourself and others, you can move on to a better, happier way of living.

RITE FOR RECONCILIATION
OF INDIVIDUAL PENITENTS[1]

Reception of the Penitent

41. When the penitent comes to confess his sins, the priest welcomes him warmly and greets him with kindness.

42. Then the penitent makes the sign of the cross which the priest may make also.

In the name of the Father, and of the Son, and of the Holy Spirit. Amen.

> *The priest invites the penitent to have trust in God, in these or similar words:*

May God, who has enlightened every heart,
help you to know your sins
and trust in his mercy.

> *The penitent answers:*

Amen.

Or:

The Lord does not wish the sinner to die   [67]
but to turn back to him and live.
Come before him with trust in his mercy.
(Ezechiel 33:11)

---

1. Chapter 1 from the *Rite of Penance,* International Committee on English in the Liturgy, Inc., copyright © 1974, pp. 31-41.

Or:

May the Lord Jesus welcome you.   [68]
He came to call sinners, not the just.
Have confidence in him.   (Luke 5:32)

Or:

May the grace of the Holy Spirit   [69]
fill your heart with light,
that you may confess your sins with loving trust
and come to know that God is merciful.

Or:

May the Lord be in your heart   [70]
and help you to confess your sins with true sorrow.

Or:

If you have sinned, do not lose heart.   [71]
We have Jesus Christ to plead for us with the Father:
he is the holy One,
the atonement for our sins
and for the sins of the whole world.   (1 John 2:1-2)

Reading of the Word of God (optional)

43. Then the priest may read or say from memory a text of Scripture which proclaims God's mercy and calls man to conversion.

> Let us look on Jesus,   [72]
> who suffered to save us
> and rose again for our justification.

Isaiah 53:4-6

**It was our infirmities that he bore,
  our sufferings that he endured,**

62

While we thought of him as stricken,
  as one smitten by God and afflicted.
But he was pierced for our offenses,
  crushed for our sins;
Upon him was the chastisement that makes us whole,
  by his stripes we were healed.
We had all gone astray like sheep,
  each following his own way;
But the LORD laid upon him the guilt of us all.

Ezechiel 11:19-20   [73]

        Let us listen to the Lord as he speaks to us:

I will give them a new heart and put a new spirit
within them; I will remove the stony heart from their
bodies, and replace it with a natural heart, so that
they will live according to my statutes, and observe
and carry out my ordinances; thus they shall be my
people and I will be their God.

Matthew 6:14-15   [74]

        Let us listen to the Lord as he speaks to us:

"If you forgive the faults of others, your heavenly
Father will forgive you yours. If you do not forgive
others, neither will your Father forgive you."

Mark 1:14-15   [75]

After John's arrest, Jesus appeared in Galilee
proclaiming the good news of God: "This is the time
of fulfillment. The reign of God is at hand! Reform
your lives and believe in the gospel!"

Do to others what you would have them do to you.
If you love those who love you, what credit is that to
you? Even sinners love those who love them. If you
do good to those who do good to you, how can you
claim any credit? Sinners do as much. If you lend to
those from whom you expect repayment, what merit is
there in it for you? Even sinners lend to sinners,
expecting to be repaid in full.

"Love your enemy and do good; lend without
expecting repayment. Then will your recompense be
great. You will rightly be called sons of the Most
High, since he himself is good to the ungrateful and
the wicked.

"Be compassionate, as your Father is
compassionate. Do not judge, and you will not be
judged. Do not condemn, and you will not be
condemned. Pardon, and you shall be pardoned.
Give, and it shall be given to you. Good measure
pressed down, shaken together, running over, will they
pour into the fold of your garment. For the measure
you measure with will be measured back to you."

The tax collectors and sinners were all gathering
around to hear him, at which the Pharisees and the
scribes murmured, "This man welcomes sinners and
eats with them." Then he addressed this parable to
them: "Who among you, if he has a hundred sheep and
loses one of them, does not leave the ninety-nine in
the wasteland and follow the lost one until he finds
it? And when he finds it, he puts it on his shoulders in
jubilation. Once arrived home, he invites friends and
neighbors in and says to them, 'Rejoice with me

because I have found my lost sheep.' I tell you, there will likewise be more joy in heaven over one repentant sinner than over ninety-nine righteous people who have no need to repent."

John 20:19-23 [78]

On the evening of that first day of the week, even though the disciples had locked the doors of the place where they were for fear of the Jews, Jesus came and stood before them. "Peace be with you," he said. When he had said this, he showed them his hands and his side. At the sight of the Lord the disciples rejoiced. "Peace be with you," he said again.

"As the Father has sent me,
so I send you."

Then he breathed on them and said:

"Receive the Holy Spirit.
If you forgive men's sins,
they are forgiven them;
if you hold them bound,
they are held bound."

Romans 5:8-9 [79]

It is precisely in this that God proves his love for us: that while we were still sinners, Christ died for us. Now that we have been justified by his blood, it is all the more certain that we shall be saved by him from God's wrath.

Ephesians 5:1-2 [80]

Be imitators of God as his dear children. Follow the

way of love, even as Christ loved you. He gave himself
for us as an offering to God, a gift of pleasing fragrance.

Colossians 1:12-14   [81]

Give thanks to the Father for having made you
worthy to share the lot of the saints in light.
He rescued us from the power of darkness and
brought us into the kingdom of his beloved Son.
Through him we have redemption, the forgiveness of
our sins.

Colossians 3:8-10, 12-17   [82]

You must put that aside now: all the anger and quick
temper, the malice, the insults, the foul language. Stop
lying to one another. What you have done is put
aside your old self with its past deeds and put on a
new man, one who grows in knowledge as he is
formed anew in the image of his Creator. Because
you are God's chosen ones, holy and beloved, clothe
yourselves with heartfelt mercy, with kindness,
humility, meekness, and patience. Bear with one
another; forgive whatever grievances you have against
one another. Forgive as the Lord has forgiven you.
Over all these virtues put on love, which binds the
rest together and makes them perfect. Christ's peace
must reign in your hearts, since as members of the
one body you have been called to that peace.
Dedicate yourselves to thankfulness. Let the word of
Christ, rich as it is, dwell in you. In wisdom made
perfect, instruct and admonish one another. Sing
gratefully to God from your hearts in psalms, hymns,
and inspired songs. Whatever you do, whether in
speech or in action, do it in the name of the Lord
Jesus. Give thanks to God the Father through him.

1 John 1:6-7, 9 [83]

If we say, "We have fellowship with him,"
while continuing to walk in darkness,
we are liars and do not act in truth.
But if we walk in light,
as he is in the light,
we have fellowship with one another,
and the blood of his Son Jesus cleanses us from all sin.
But if we acknowledge our sins,
he who is just can be trusted
to forgive our sins
and cleanse us from every wrong.

[84]

A reading may also be chosen from those given in nos. 101-201 for the reconciliation of several penitents. The priest and penitent may choose other readings from scripture.

Confession of Sins and Acceptance of Satisfaction

44. Where it is the custom, the penitent says a general formula for confession (for example, I confess to almighty God) before he confesses his sins.

If necessary, the priest helps the penitent to make an integral confession and gives him suitable counsel. He urges him to be sorry for his faults, reminding him that through the sacrament of penance the Christian dies and rises with Christ and is thus renewed in the paschal mystery. The priest proposes an act of penance which the penitent accepts to make satisfaction for sin and to amend his life.

The priest should make sure that he adapts his counsel to the penitent's circumstances.

Prayer of the Penitent and Absolution

45. The priest then asks the penitent to express his sorrow, which the penitent may do in these or similar words:

My God,
I am sorry for my sins with all my heart.
In choosing to do wrong
and failing to do good,
I have sinned against you
whom I should love above all things.
I firmly intend, with your help,
to do penance,
to sin no more,
and to avoid whatever leads me to sin.
Our Savior Jesus Christ
suffered and died for us.
In his name, my God, have mercy.

Or:

Remember, O Lord, your compassion and   [85]
    mercy which you showed long ago.
Do not recall the sins and failings of my youth.
In your mercy remember me, Lord, because of your
    goodness. (Psalm 25:6-7)

Or:

Wash me from my guilt   [86]
and cleanse me of my sin.
I acknowledge my offense;
my sin is before me always. (Ps 51:4-5)

Or:

Father, I have sinned against you   [87]
and am not worthy to be called your son.
Be merciful to me, a sinner. (Luke 15:18; 18:13)

Or:

Father of mercy,   [88]
like the prodigal son
I return to you and say:
"I have sinned against you
and am no longer worthy to be called your son."
Christ Jesus, Savior of the world,
I pray with the repentant thief
to whom you promised Paradise:
"Lord, remember me in your kingdom."
Holy Spirit, fountain of love,
I call on you with trust:
"Purify my heart,
and help me to walk as a child of light."

Or:

Lord Jesus,   [89]
you opened the eyes of the blind,
healed the sick,
forgave the sinful woman,
and after Peter's denial confirmed him in your love.
Listen to my prayer:
forgive all my sins,
renew your love in my heart,
help me to live in perfect unity with my fellow
      Christians
that I may proclaim your saving power to all the world.

Or:

Lord Jesus,   [90]
you chose to be called the friend of sinners.
By your saving death and resurrection
free me from my sins.
May your peace take root in my heart
and bring forth a harvest
of love, holiness, and truth.

Or:

Lord Jesus Christ,   [91]
you are the Lamb of God;
you take away the sins of the world.
Through the grace of the Holy Spirit
restore me to friendship with your Father,
cleanse me from every stain of sin
in the blood you shed for me,
and raise me to new life
for the glory of your name.

Or:

Lord God,   [92]
in your goodness have mercy on me:
do not look on my sins,
but take away all my guilt.
Create in me a clean heart
and renew within me an upright spirit.

Or:

Lord Jesus, Son of God,
have mercy on me, a sinner.

*46. Then the priest extends his hands over the peni-
tent's head (or at least extends his right hand) and says:*

God, the Father of mercies,
through the death and resurrection of his Son
has reconciled the world to himself
and sent the Holy Spirit among us
for the forgiveness of sins;
through the ministry of the Church
may God give you pardon and peace,
and I absolve you from your sins
in the name of the Father, and of the Son,+
and of the Holy Spirit.

   The penitent answers:

Amen.

Proclamation of Praise of God and Dismissal

47. After the absolution, the priest continues:

Give thanks to the Lord, for he is good.

> *The penitent concludes:*

His mercy endures for ever.

> *Then the priest dismisses the penitent who has been reconciled, saying:*

The Lord has freed you from your sins. Go in peace.

Or: [93]

May the Passion of our Lord Jesus Christ,
the intercession of the Blessed Virgin Mary
    and of all the saints,
whatever good you do and suffering you endure,
heal your sins,
help you to grow in holiness,
and reward you with eternal life.
Go in peace.

Or:

The Lord has freed you from sin.
May he bring you safely to his kingdom in heaven.
Glory to him for ever.

Amen.

Or:

Blessed are those
whose sins have been forgiven,
whose evil deeds have been forgotten.
Rejoice in the Lord,
and go in peace.

Or:

Go in peace,
and proclaim to the world
the wonderful works of God,
who has brought you salvation.

Some Sample Confessions of Sin

A. "Forgive me, Father. I'm a married man. It's
been a month since my last confession. I got angry
and lost my temper at the children. This happens
often now when I get home from work. I'm
tired and I don't want to be bothered.

"I know this is selfish. My anger just makes
things worse. I'll try to spend more time with
the kids and listen to them instead of yell. Where
should I start? Have you any advice?"[2]

B. "Help me, Father, to make a good confession.
I'm a fourth grade girl and it has been three
months since my last confession.

"I have a brother in the second grade and we
are always getting into fights and then my mom
and dad get mad at us. I think I fight with him
so much because I feel he's my dad's favorite and
I'm jealous of him. I'm going to try to think
more about the attention that dad gives to me
and forget about noticing all the attention that my
brother gets.

"I am sorry for this sin and will try to change
my attitude toward my brother."

---

2. Sample confession in *I Confess* by Francis J. Buckley, S.J.,
Ave Maria Press, Notre Dame, Indiana, 1972, pp. 86-87.

Step 5:
Penances for the Past and for the Future

The confessor imposes upon you a penance or satis-faction for your sins as the final step in this sacrament of reconciliation. Designed to repair the harm done and to heal the wounds caused by these misdeeds, it is also intended to help you improve in the days ahead. He will, as your penance, assign a prayer or prayers, propose some action related to a particular sin con-fessed, or designate one, perhaps several of the read-ings below. The priest may even offer to read with you the biblical passage selected before pronouncing the words of absolution and forgiveness.

1. Happiness of the Forgiven Sinner

PSALM 32

I

Happy is he whose fault is taken away,
   whose sin is covered.
Happy the man to whom the LORD imputes not guilt,
   in whose spirit there is no guile.

II

As long as I would not speak, my bones wasted away
   with my groaning all the day,
For day and night your hand was heavy upon me;

my strength was dried up as by the heat of summer.
Then I acknowledged my sin to you,
 my guilt I covered not.
I said, "I confess my faults to the LORD,"
 and you took away the guilt of my sin.
For this shall every faithful man pray to you
 in time of stress.
Though deep waters overflow,
 they shall not reach him.
You are my shelter; from distress you will preserve me;
 with glad cries of freedom you will ring me round.

III

I will instruct you and show you the way you should
 walk;
 I will counsel you, keeping my eye on you.
Be not senseless like horses or mules:
 with bit and bridle their temper must be curbed,
 else they will not come near you.

IV

Many are the sorrows of the wicked,
 but kindness surrounds him who trusts in the LORD.
Be glad in the LORD and rejoice, you just;
 exult, all you upright of heart.

2. The Miserere: A Prayer of Repentance

PSALM 51

A

Have mercy on me, O God, in your goodness;
 in the greatness of your compassion wipe out my
 offense.

Thoroughly wash me from my guilt
 and of my sin cleanse me.

B

I

For I acknowledge my offense,
 and my sin is before me always;
"Against you only have I sinned,
 and done what is evil in your sight"—
That you may be justified in your sentence,
 vindicated when you condemn.
Indeed, in guilt was I born,
 and in sin my mother conceived me;
Behold, you are pleased with sincerity of heart,
 and in my inmost being you teach me wisdom.

II

Cleanse me of sin with hyssop, that I may be purified;
 wash me, and I shall be whiter than snow.
Let me hear the sounds of joy and gladness;
 the bones you have crushed shall rejoice.
Turn away your face from my sins,
 and blot out all my guilt.

III

A clean heart create for me, O God,
 and a steadfast spirit renew within me.
Cast me not out from your presence,
 and your holy spirit take not from me.
Give me back the joy of your salvation,
 and a willing spirit sustain in me.

IV

I will teach transgressors your ways,
    and sinners shall return to you.
Free me from blood guilt, O God, my saving God;
    then my tongue shall revel in your justice.
O Lord, open my lips,
    and my mouth shall proclaim your praise.
For you are not pleased with sacrifices;
    should I offer a holocaust, you would not accept it.
My sacrifice, O God, is a contrite spirit;
    a heart contrite and humbled, O God, you will not
      spurn.

C

Be bountiful, O LORD, to Zion in your kindness
    by rebuilding the walls of Jerusalem;
Then shall you be pleased with due sacrifices,
    burnt offerings and holocausts;
    then shall they offer up bullocks on your altar.

3. A Distressed Sinner's Prayer for Help

PSALM 143

I

O LORD, hear my prayer;
    hearken to my pleading in your faithfulness;
    in your justice answer me.
And enter not into judgment with your servant,
    for before you no living man is just.

II

For the enemy pursues me;
   he has crushed my life to the ground;
   he has left me dwelling in the dark, like those long
      dead.
And my spirit is faint within me,
   my heart within me is appalled.
I remember the days of old;
   I meditate on all your doings,
   the works of your hands I ponder.
I stretch out my hands to you;
   my soul thirsts for you like parched land.

III

Hasten to answer me, O LORD, for my spirit fails me.
Hide not your face from me
   lest I become like those who go down into the pit.
At dawn let me hear of your kindness,
   for in you I trust.
Show me the way in which I should walk,
   for to you I lift up my soul.
Rescue me from my enemies, O LORD,
   for in you I hope.

4. The Beatitudes in Luke

Coming down the mountain with them, he stopped
at a level stretch where there were many of his
disciples; a large crowd of people was with them from
all Judea and Jerusalem and the coast of Tyre and Sidon,
people who came to hear him and be healed of their
diseases. Those who were troubled with unclean
spirits were cured; indeed, the whole crowd was
trying to touch him because power went out from him
which cured all. Then, raising his eyes to his disciples,
he said:

77

"Blest are you poor; the reign of God is yours.
Blest are you who hunger; you shall be filled.
Blest are you who are weeping; you shall laugh.
"Blest shall you be when men hate you, when they
ostracize you and insult you and proscribe your
name as evil because of the Son of Man. On the
day they do so, rejoice and exult, for your reward
shall be great in heaven. Thus it was that their fathers
treated the prophets.

"But woe to you rich, for your consolation is now.
Woe to you who are full; you shall go hungry.
Woe to you who laugh now; you shall weep in your
    grief.

"Woe to you when all speak well of you. Their fathers
treated the false prophets in just this way."
—Luke 6:17-26

The Beatitudes in Matthew

When he saw the crowds he went up on the
mountainside. After he had sat down his disciples
gathered around him, and he began to teach them:

"How blest are the poor in spirit:
    the reign of God is theirs.
Blest too are the sorrowing; they shall be consoled.
[Blest are the lowly; they shall inherit the land.]
Blest are they who hunger and thirst for holiness;
they shall have their fill.
Blest are they who show mercy; mercy shall be theirs.
Blest are the single-hearted for they shall see God.
Blest too the peacemakers; they shall be called sons of
    God.
Blest are those persecuted for holiness' sake; the reign
    of God is theirs.
Blest are you when they insult you and persecute you

78

and utter every kind of slander against you because
of me.
Be glad and rejoice, for your reward is great in
    heaven;
they persecuted the prophets before you in the
    very same way."—Matthew 5:1-12

5. Jesus' Teaching About the Cross

Jesus then said to his disciples: "If a man wishes to
come after me, he must deny his very self, take up his
cross, and begin to follow in my footsteps. Whoever
would save his life will lose it, but whoever loses his life
for my sake will find it. What profit would a man
show if he were to gain the whole world and destroy
himself in the process? What can a man offer in
exchange for his very self? The Son of Man will come
with his Father's glory accompanied by his angels.
When he does, he will repay each man according to
his conduct. I assure you, among those standing here
there are some who will not experience death before
they see the Son of Man come in his kingship."
—Matthew 16:24-28

6. The Need for Watchfulness

"The coming of the Son of Man will repeat what
happened in Noah's time. In the days before the flood
people were eating and drinking, marrying and being
married, right up to the day Noah entered the ark.
They were totally unconcerned until the flood came
and destroyed them. So will it be at the coming of the
Son of Man. Two men will be out in the field; one will
be taken and one will be left. Two women will be
grinding meal; one will be taken and one will be left.
Stay awake, therefore! You cannot know the day your
Lord is coming.

"Be sure of this: if the owner of the house knew when the thief was coming he would keep a watchful eye and not allow his house to be broken into. You must be prepared in the same way. The Son of Man is coming at the time you least expect. Who is the faithful, farsighted servant whom the master has put in charge of his household to dispense food at need? Happy that servant whom his master discovers at work on his return! I assure you, he will put him in charge of all his property. But if the servant is worthless and tells himself, 'My master is a long time in coming,' and begins to beat his fellow servants, to eat and drink with drunkards, that man's master will return when he is not ready and least expects him. He will punish him severely and settle with him as is done with hypocrites. There will be wailing then and grinding of teeth."—Matthew 24:37-51

7. Love for Others, Especially Our Enemies

"To you who hear me, I say: Love your enemies, do good to those who hate you; bless those who curse you and pray for those who maltreat you. When someone slaps you on one cheek, turn and give him the other; when someone takes your coat, let him have your shirt as well. Give to all who beg from you. When a man takes what is yours, do not demand it back. Do to others what you would have them do to you. If you love those who love you, what credit is that to you? Even sinners love those who love them. If you do good to those who do good to you, how can you claim any credit? Sinners do as much. If you lend to those from whom you expect repayment, what merit is there in it for you? Even sinners lend to sinners, expecting to be repaid in full.

"Love your enemy and do good; lend without expecting repayment. Then will your recompense be great. You will rightly be called sons of the Most High, since he himself is good to the ungrateful and the wicked.

"Be compassionate, as your Father is compassionate. Do not judge, and you will not be judged. Do not condemn, and you will not be condemned. Pardon, and you shall be pardoned. Give, and it shall be given to you. Good measure pressed down, shaken together, running over, will they pour into the fold of your garment. For the measure you measure with will be measured back to you."
—Luke 6:27-38

8. Christ's Promise of Peace

"I will not leave you orphaned;
I will come back to you.
A little while now and the world will see me no more;
but you see me
as one who has life, and you will have life.
On that day you will know
that I am in my Father,
and you in me, and I in you.
He who obeys the commandments he has from me
is the man who loves me;
and he who loves me will be loved by my Father.
I too will love him
and reveal myself to him."

Judas (not Judas Iscariot) said to him, "Lord, why is it that you will reveal yourself to us and not to the world?" Jesus answered:

"Anyone who loves me
will be true to my word,
and my Father will love him;
we will come to him

and make our dwelling place with him.
He who does not love me does not keep my words.
Yet the word you hear is not mine;
it comes from the Father who sent me.
This much have I told you while I was still with you;
the Paraclete, the Holy Spirit
whom the Father will send in my name,
will instruct you in everything,
and remind you of all that I told you.
'Peace' is my farewell to you,
my peace is my gift to you;
I do not give it to you as the world gives peace.
Do not be distressed or fearful.
You have heard me say,
'I go away for a while, and I come back to you.'
If you truly loved me
you would rejoice to have me go to the Father,
for the Father is greater than I.
I tell you this now, before it takes place,
so that when it takes place you may believe.
I shall not go on speaking to you longer;
the Prince of this world is at hand.
He has no hold on me,
but the world must know that I love the Father
and do as the Father has commanded me.
Come, then! Let us be on our way."—John 14:18-31

9. The Vine and the Branches

"I am the true vine
and my Father is the vinegrower.
He prunes away
every barren branch,
but the fruitful ones
he trims clean
to increase their yield.
You are clean already,

thanks to the word I have spoken to you.
Live on in me, as I do in you.
No more than a branch can bear fruit of itself
apart from the vine,
can you bear fruit
apart from me.
I am the vine, you are the branches.
He who lives in me and I in him,
will produce abundantly,
for apart from me you can do nothing.
A man who does not live in me
is like a withered, rejected branch,
picked up to be thrown in the fire and burnt.
If you live in me,
and my words stay part of you,
you may ask what you will—
it will be done for you.
My Father has been glorified
in your bearing much fruit
and becoming my disciples."—John 15:1-8

10. The Lord's Command to Love

"As the Father has loved me,
so I have loved you.
Live on in my love.
You will live in my love
if you keep my commandments,
even as I have kept my Father's commandments,
and live in his love.
All this I tell you
that my joy may be yours
and your joy may be complete.
This is my commandment:
love one another
as I have loved you.
There is no greater love than this:

to lay down one's life for one's friends.
You are my friends
if you do what I command you.
I no longer speak of you as slaves,
for a slave does not know what his master is about.
Instead, I call you friends,
since I have made known to you all that I heard from
   my Father.
It was not you who chose me,
it was I who chose you
to go forth and bear fruit.
Your fruit must endure,
so that all you ask the Father in my name
he will give you.
The command I give you is this,
that you love one another."—John 15:9-17

11. Dead to Sin, Alive in God

What, then, are we to say? "Let us continue in sin that
grace may abound"? Certainly not! How can we who
died to sin go on living in it? Are you not aware that
we who were baptized into Christ Jesus were baptized
into his death? Through baptism into his death we
were buried with him, so that, just as Christ was raised
from the dead by the glory of the Father, we too
might live a new life. If we have been united with him
through likeness to his death, so shall we be through
a like resurrection. This we know: our old self was
crucified with him so that the sinful body might be
destroyed and we might be slaves to sin no longer. A
man who is dead has been freed from sin. If we have
died with Christ, we believe that we are also to live
with him. We know that Christ, once raised from the
dead, will never die again; death has no more power
over him. His death was death to sin, once for all;
his life is life for God. In the same way, you must

consider yourselves dead to sin but alive for God in Christ Jesus.

Do not, therefore, let sin rule your mortal body and make you obey its lusts; no more shall you offer the members of your body to sin as weapons for evil. Rather, offer yourselves to God as men who have come back from the dead to life, and your bodies to God as weapons for justice. Sin will no longer have power over you; you are now under grace, not under the law.—Romans 6:1-14

12. Freed from Sin, Slaves for God

What does all this lead to? Just because we are not under the law but under grace, are we free to sin? By no means! You must realize that, when you offer yourselves to someone as obedient slaves, you are the slaves of the one you obey, whether yours is the slavery of sin, which leads to death, or of obedience, which leads to justice. Thanks be to God, though once you were slaves of sin, you sincerely obeyed that rule of teaching which was imparted to you; freed from your sin, you became slaves of justice. (I use the following example from human affairs because of your weak human nature.) Just as formerly you enslaved your bodies to impurity and licentiousness for their degradation, make them now the servants of justice for their sanctification. When you were slaves of sin, you had freedom from justice. What benefit did you then enjoy? Things you are now ashamed of, all of them tending toward death. But now that you are freed from sin and have become slaves of God, your benefit is sanctification as you tend toward eternal life. The wages of sin is death, but the gift of God is eternal life in Christ Jesus our Lord.
—Romans 6:15-23

13. Conflict Within Us Between Good and Evil

We know that the law is spiritual, whereas I am weak flesh sold into the slavery of sin. I cannot even understand my own actions. I do not do what I want to do but what I hate. When I act against my own will, by that very fact I agree that the law is good. This indicates that it is not I who do it but sin which resides in me. I know that no good dwells in me, that is, in my flesh; the desire to do right is there but not the power. What happens is that I do, not the good I will to do, but the evil I do not intend. But if I do what is against my will, it is not I who do it, but sin which dwells in me. This means that even though I want to do what is right, a law that leads to wrong-doing is always ready at hand. My inner self agrees with the law of God, but I see in my body's members another law at war with the law of my mind; this makes me the prisoner of the law of sin in my members. What a wretched man I am! Who can free me from this body under the power of death? All praise to God, through Jesus Christ our Lord! So with my mind I serve the law of God but with my flesh the law of sin.—Romans 7:14-25

14. God's Help for Our Weakness

The Spirit too helps us in our weakness, for we do not know how to pray as we ought; but the Spirit himself makes intercession for us with groanings that cannot be expressed in speech. He who searches hearts knows what the Spirit means, for the Spirit intercedes for the saints as God himself wills.

We know that God makes all things work together for the good of those who have been called according to his decree. Those whom he foreknew he predestined to share the image of his Son, that the

Son might be the first-born of many brothers. Those he predestined he likewise called; those he called he also justified; and those he justified he in turn glorified. What shall we say after that? If God is for us, who can be against us? Is it possible that he who . did not spare his own Son but handed him over for the sake of us all will not grant us all things besides? —Romans 8:26-32

15. Clinging to Christ in the Midst of Difficulties

What shall we say after that? If God is for us, who can be against us? Is it possible that he who did not spare his own Son but handed him over for the sake of us all will not grant us all things besides? Who shall bring a charge against God's chosen ones? God, who justifies? Who shall condemn them? Christ Jesus, who died or rather was raised up, who is at the right hand of God and who intercedes for us? Who will separate us from the love of Christ? Trial, or distress, or persecution, or hunger, or nakedness, or danger, or the sword? As Scripture says: "For your sake we are being slain all the day long; we are looked upon as sheep to be slaughtered." Yet in all this we are more than conquerors because of him who has loved us. For I am certain that neither death nor life, neither angels nor principalities, neither the present nor the future, nor powers, neither height nor depth nor any other creature, will be able to separate us from the love of God that comes to us in Christ Jesus, our Lord.—Romans 8:31-39

16. A Call to Love Others

And now, brothers, I beg you through the mercy of God to offer your bodies as a living sacrifice holy and acceptable to God, your spiritual worship. Do not conform yourselves to this age but be transformed by the renewal of your mind, so that you may judge what is God's will, what is good, pleasing and perfect.

Your love must be sincere. Detest what is evil, cling to what is good. Love one another with the affection of brothers. Anticipate each other in showing respect. Do not grow slack but be fervent in spirit; he whom you serve is the Lord. Rejoice in hope, be patient under trial, persevere in prayer. Look on the needs of the saints as your own; be generous in offering hospitality. Bless your persecutors; bless and do not curse them. Rejoice with those who rejoice, weep with those who weep. Have the same attitude toward all. Put away ambitious thoughts and associate with those who are lowly. Do not be wise in your own estimation. Never repay injury with injury. See that your conduct is honorable in the eyes of all. If possible, live peaceably with everyone. Beloved, do not avenge yourselves; leave that to God's wrath, for it is written: " 'Vengeance is mine; I will repay,' says the Lord." But "if your enemy is hungry, feed him; if he is thirsty, give him something to drink; by doing this you will heap burning coals upon his head." Do not be conquered by evil but conquer evil with good.—Romans 12:1-2, 9-21

17. Our Salvation Is Due to God's Loving Mercy

You were dead because of your sins and offenses, as you gave allegiance to the present age and to the prince of the air, that spirit who is even now at work among the rebellious. All of us were once of their company; we lived at the level of the flesh, following every whim and fancy, and so by nature deserved God's wrath like the rest. But God is rich in mercy; because of his great love for us he brought us to life with Christ when we were dead in sin. By this favor

88

you were saved. Both with and in Christ Jesus he raised us up and gave us a place in the heavens, that in the ages to come he might display the great wealth of his favor, manifested by his kindness to us in Christ Jesus. I repeat, it is owing to his favor that salvation is yours through faith. This is not your own doing, it is God's gift; neither is it a reward for anything you have accomplished, so let no one pride himself on it. We are truly his handiwork, created in Christ Jesus to lead the life of good deeds which God prepared for us in advance.—Ephesians 2:1-10

18. An Exhortation to Live in Christian Unity

I plead with you, then, as a prisoner for the Lord, to live a life worthy of the calling you have received, with perfect humility, meekness, and patience, bearing with one another lovingly. Make every effort to preserve the unity which has the Spirit as its origin and peace as its binding force. There is but one body and one Spirit, just as there is but one hope given all of you by your call. There is one Lord, one faith, one baptism; one God and Father of all, who is over all, and works through all, and is in all.
Each of us has received God's favor in the measure in which Christ bestows it.—Ephesians 4:1-7

19. Some Vices To Be Avoided

I declare and solemnly attest in the Lord that you must no longer live as the pagans do—their minds empty, their understanding darkened. They are estranged from a life in God because of their ignorance and their resistance; without remorse they have abandoned themselves to lust and the indulgence of every sort of lewd conduct. That is not what you learned when you learned Christ! I am supposing, of course, that he has been preached and taught to you in accord with the truth that is in Jesus: namely, that you must lay aside your former way of life and old self which deteriorates through illusion and desire, and acquire a fresh, spiritual way of thinking. You must put on that new man created in God's image, whose justice and holiness are born of truth.

See to it, then, that you put an end to lying; let everyone speak the truth to his neighbor, for we are members of one another. If you are angry, let it be without sin. The sun must not go down on your wrath; do not give the devil a chance to work on you. The man who has been stealing must steal no longer; rather, let him work with his hands at honest labor so that he will have something to share with those in need. Never let evil talk pass your lips; say only the good things men need to hear, things that will really help them. Do nothing to sadden the Holy Spirit with whom you were sealed against the day of redemption. Get rid of all bitterness, all passion and anger, harsh words, slander, and malice of every kind. In place of these, be kind to one another, compassionate, and mutually forgiving, just as God has forgiven you in Christ.—Ephesians 4:17-32

20. The Christian's Need for Continued Progress

Ever since we heard this we have been praying for you unceasingly and asking that you may attain full knowledge of his will through perfect wisdom and spiritual insight. Then you will lead a life worthy of the Lord and pleasing to him in every way. You will multiply good works of every sort and grow in the knowledge of God. By the might of his glory you will be endowed with the strength needed to stand fast, even to endure joyfully whatever may come, giving thanks to the Father for having made you worthy to

share the lot of the saints in light. He rescued us from the power of darkness and brought us into the kingdom of his beloved Son. Through him we have redemption, the forgiveness of our sins.
—Colossians 1:9-14

21. Casting Aside the Old Self and Putting on the New Man in Christ

Since you have been raised up in company with Christ, set your heart on what pertains to higher realms where Christ is seated at God's right hand. Be intent on things above rather than on things of earth. After all, you have died! Your life is hidden now with Christ in God. When Christ our life appears, then you shall appear with him in glory.

Put to death whatever in your nature is rooted in earth: fornication, uncleanness, passion, evil desires, and that lust which is idolatry. These are the sins which provoke God's wrath. Your own conduct was once of this sort, when these sins were your very life. You must put that aside now: all the anger and quick temper, the malice, the insults, the foul language. Stop lying to one another. What you have done is put aside your old self with its past deeds and put on a new man, one who grows in knowledge as he is formed anew in the image of his Creator. There is no Greek or Jew here, circumcised or uncircumcised, foreigner, Scythian, slave, or freeman. Rather, Christ is everything in all of you.

Because you are God's chosen ones, holy and beloved, clothe yourselves with heartfelt mercy, with kindness, humility, meekness, and patience. Bear with one another; forgive whatever grievances you have against one another. Forgive as the Lord has forgiven you. Over all these virtues put on love, which binds the rest together and makes them perfect. Christ's peace

91

must reign in your hearts, since as members of the one body you have been called to that peace. Dedicate yourselves to thankfulness. Let the word of Christ, rich as it is, dwell in you. In wisdom made perfect, instruct and admonish one another. Sing gratefully to God from your hearts in psalms, hymns, and inspired songs. Whatever you do, whether in speech or in action, do it in the name of the Lord Jesus. Give thanks to God the Father through him.
—Colossians 3:1-17

22. God Calls Us to Holiness, Not Immorality

Now, my brothers, we beg and exhort you in the Lord Jesus that even as you learned from us how to conduct yourselves in a way pleasing to God—which you are indeed doing—so you must learn to make still greater progress. You know the instructions we gave you in the Lord Jesus. It is God's will that you grow in holiness: that you abstain from immorality, each of you guarding his member in sanctity and honor, not in passionate desire as do the Gentiles who know not God; and that each refrain from over-reaching or cheating his brother in the matter at hand; for the Lord is an avenger of all such things, as we once indicated to you by our testimony. God has not called us to immorality but to holiness, hence, whoever rejects these instructions rejects, not man, but God who sends his Holy Spirit upon you.

As regards brotherly love, there is no need for me to write you. God himself has taught you to love one another, and this you are doing with respect to all the brothers throughout Macedonia. Yet we exhort you to even greater progress, brothers. Make it a point of honor to remain at peace and attend to your own affairs. Work with your hands as we directed you to do, so that you will give good example to outsiders and want for nothing.—1 Thessalonians 4:1-12

23. Hearing the Lord's Word and Acting on It

Humbly welcome the word that has taken root in you, with its power to save you. Act on this word. If all you do is listen to it, you are deceiving yourselves.

A man who listens to God's word but does not put it into practice is like a man who looks into a mirror at the face he was born with; he looks at himself, then goes off and promptly forgets what he looked like. There is, on the other hand, the man who peers into freedom's ideal law and abides by it. He is no forgetful listener, but one who carries out the law in practice. Blest will this man be in whatever he does.

If a man who does not control his tongue imagines that he is devout, he is self-deceived; his worship is pointless. Looking after orphans and widows in their distress and keeping oneself unspotted by the world make for pure worship without stain before our God and Father.—James 1:21-27

24. Faith and Good Works

My brothers, what good is it to profess faith without practicing it? Such faith has no power to save one, has it? If a brother or sister has nothing to wear and no food for the day, and you say to them, "Goodbye and good luck! Keep warm and well fed," but do not meet their bodily needs, what good is that? So it is with the faith that does nothing in practice. It is thoroughly lifeless.

To such a person one might say, "You have faith and I have works—is that it?" Show me your faith without works, and I will show you the faith that underlies my works! Do you believe that God is one? You are quite right. The demons believe that, and shudder. Do you want proof, you ignoramus, that without works faith is idle? Was not our father

Abraham justified by his works when he offered his
son Isaac on the altar? There you see proof that faith
was both assisting his works and implemented by his
works. You also see how the Scripture was fulfilled
which says, "Abraham believed God, and it was
credited to him as justice"; for this he received the
title "God's friend."

You must perceive that a person is justified by his
works and not by faith alone. Rahab the harlot will
illustrate the point. Was she not justified by her works
when she harbored the messengers and sent them out
by a different route? Be assured, then, that faith
without works is as dead as a body without breath.
—James 2:14-26

25. Command to Love in Deed and Truth

See what love the Father has bestowed on us
in letting us be called children of God!
Yet that is what we are.
The reason the world does not recognize us
is that it never recognized the Son.
Dearly beloved,
we are God's children now;
what we shall later be has not yet come to light.
We know that when it comes to light
we shall be like him,
for we shall see him as he is.
Everyone who has this hope based on him
keeps himself pure, as he is pure.

Everyone who sins acts lawlessly,
for sin is lawlessness.
You know well that the reason he revealed himself
was to take away sins;
in him there is nothing sinful.
The man who remains in him does not sin.

The man who sins has not seen him
or known him.
Little ones,
let no one deceive you;
the man who acts in holiness is holy indeed,
even as the Son is holy.
The man who sins belongs to the devil,
because the devil is a sinner from the beginning.
It was to destroy the devil's works
that the Son of God revealed himself.

No one begotten of God acts sinfully
because he remains of God's stock;
he cannot sin
because he is begotten of God.
That is the way to see who are God's children,
and who are the devil's.
No one whose actions are unholy belongs to God,
nor anyone who fails to love his brother.
This, remember, is the message
you heard from the beginning:
we should love one another.
We should not follow the example of Cain
who belonged to the evil one
and killed his brother.
Why did he kill him?
Because his own deeds were wicked
while his brother's were just.
No need, then, brothers, to be surprised
if the world hates you.
That we have passed from death to life we know
because we love the brothers.
The man who does not love is among the living dead.
Anyone who hates his brother is a murderer,
and you know that eternal life
abides in no murderer's heart.
The way we came to understand love

was that he laid down his life for us;
we too must lay down our lives for our brothers.
I ask you, how can God's love survive in a man
who has enough of this world's goods
yet closes his heart to his brother
when he sees him in need?
Little children,
let us love in deed and in truth
and not merely talk about it.
This is our way of knowing we are committed to the
    truth
and are at peace before him
no matter what our consciences may charge us with;
for God is greater than our hearts
and all is known to him.
Beloved,
if our consciences have nothing to charge us with,
we can be sure that God is with us
and that we will receive at his hands
whatever we ask.
Why? Because we are keeping his commandments
and doing what is pleasing in his sight.
His commandment is this:
we are to believe in the name of his Son, Jesus Christ,
and are to love one another as he commanded us.
Those who keep his commandments remain in him
and he in them.
And this is how we know that he remains in us:
from the Spirit that he gave us.—1 John 3:1-24

26. Love of God Through Love of Neighbor

Beloved,
let us love one another
because love is of God;
everyone who loves is begotten of God
and has knowledge of God.

The man without love has known nothing of God,
for God is love.
God's love was revealed in our midst in this way:
he sent his only Son to the world
that we might have life through him.
Love, then, consists in this:
not that we have loved God,
but that he has loved us
and has sent his Son as an offering for our sins.
Beloved,
if God has loved us so,
we must have the same love for one another.
No one has ever seen God.
Yet if we love one another
God dwells in us,
and his love is brought to perfection in us.
The way we know we remain in him
and he in us
is that he has given us of his Spirit.
We have seen for ourselves, and can testify,
that the Father has sent the Son as savior of the world.
When anyone acknowledges that Jesus is the Son of
     God,
God dwells in him
and he in God.
We have come to know and to believe
   in the love God has for us.
God is love,
and he who abides in love
abides in God,
and God in him.
Our love is brought to perfection in this,
that we should have confidence on the day of
     judgment;
for our relation to this world is just like his.
Love has no room for fear;
rather, perfect love casts out all fear.

And since fear has to do with punishment,
love is not yet perfect in one who is afraid.
We, for our part, love
because he first loved us.
If anyone says, "My love is fixed on God,"
yet hates his brother,
he is a liar.
One who has no love for the brother he has seen
cannot love the God he has not seen.
The commandment we have from him is this:
Whoever loves God must also love his brother.
—1 John 4:7-21

27. The Greatest of These Is Love

Now I will show you the way which surpasses all the
others. If I speak with human tongues and angelic
as well, but do not have love, I am a noisy gong, a
clanging cymbal. If I have the gift of prophecy and,
with full knowledge, comprehend all mysteries, if I
have faith great enough to move mountains, but have
not love, I am nothing. If I give everything I have to
feed the poor and hand over my body to be burned,
but have not love, I gain nothing.

Love is patient; love is kind. Love is not jealous,
it does not put on airs, it is not snobbish. Love is never
rude, it is not self-seeking, it is not prone to anger;
neither does it brood over injuries. Love does not
rejoice in what is wrong but rejoices with the truth.
There is no limit to love's forbearance, to its trust, its
hope, its power to endure.

Love never fails. Prophecies will cease, tongues
will be silent, knowledge will pass away. Our knowledge is imperfect and our prophesying is imperfect.
When the perfect comes, the imperfect will pass away.
When I was a child I used to talk like a child, think
like a child, reason like a child. When I became a man

I put childish ways aside. Now we see indistinctly, as in a mirror; then we shall see face to face. My knowledge is imperfect now; then I shall know even as I am known. There are in the end three things that last: faith, hope, and love, and the greatest of these is love.—1 Corinthians 13:1-13

28. The Need and Reward of Repentance

Cry out full-throated and unsparingly,
    lift up your voice like a trumpet blast;
Tell my people their wickedness,
    and the house of Jacob their sins.
They seek me day after day,
    and desire to know my ways,
Like a nation that has done what is just
    and not abandoned the law of their God;
They ask me to declare what is due them,
    pleased to gain access to God.
"Why do we fast, and you do not see it?
    afflict ourselves, and you take no note of it?"
Lo, on your fast day you carry out your own pursuits,
    and drive all your laborers.
Yes, your fast ends in quarreling and fighting,
    striking with wicked claw.
Would that today you might fast
    so as to make your voice heard on high!
Is this the manner of fasting I wish,
    of keeping a day of penance:
That a man bow his head like a reed,
    and lie in sackcloth and ashes?
Do you call this a fast,
    a day acceptable to the LORD?
This, rather, is the fasting that I wish:
    releasing those bound unjustly,
    untying the thongs of the yoke;
Setting free the oppressed,

breaking every yoke;
Sharing your bread with the hungry,
  sheltering the oppressed and the homeless;
Clothing the naked when you see them,
  and not turning your back on your own.
Then your light shall break forth like the dawn,
  and your wound shall quickly be healed;
Your vindication shall go before you,
  and the glory of the LORD shall be your rear guard.
Then you shall call, and the LORD will answer,
  you shall cry for help, and he will say: Here I am!
If you remove from your midst oppression,
  false accusation and malicious speech;
If you bestow your bread on the hungry
  and satisfy the afflicted;
Then light shall rise for you in the darkness,
  and the gloom shall become for you like midday;
Then the LORD will guide you always
  and give you plenty even on the parched land.
He will renew your strength,
  and you shall be like a watered garden,
  like a spring whose water never fails.—Isaiah 58:1-11

29. Some Common Catholic Prayers

THE APOSTLES' CREED

I believe in God, the Father almighty,
   creator of heaven and earth.

I believe in Jesus Christ, his only Son, Our Lord.
   He was conceived by the power of the Holy Spirit
      and born of the Virgin Mary.
   He suffered under Pontius Pilate,
      was crucified, died, and was buried.
He descended to the dead.
On the third day he rose again.
   He ascended into heaven,
      and is seated at the right hand of the Father.
   He will come again to judge the living and the dead.

I believe in the Holy Spirit,
   the holy catholic Church,
   the communion of saints,
   the forgiveness of sins,
   the resurrection of the body,
   and the life everlasting.

THE OUR FATHER

Our Father, who art in heaven,
hallowed be thy name:
thy kingdom come;
thy will be done on earth as it is in heaven.
Give us this day our daily bread;
and forgive us our trespasses
as we forgive those who trespass against us;
and lead us not into temptation,

but deliver us from evil.

For the kingdom, the power, and the glory are yours
    now and for ever.

GLORY TO THE FATHER

Glory to the Father, and to the Son, and
      to the Holy Spirit:
  as it was in the beginning, is now, and will be for
     ever. Amen.

THE HAIL MARY

Hail, Mary, full of grace, the Lord is with you.
Blessed are you among women,
And blessed is the fruit of your womb, Jesus.
Holy Mary, Mother of God, pray for us sinners,
     now and at the hour of our death. Amen.